SEEKING TO UNDERSTAND

SEEKING TO UNDERSTAND

A JOURNEY INTO DISABILITY STUDIES AND LIBRARIES

Robin Brown and Scott Sheidlower

Library Juice Press
Sacramento, CA

Published by Library Juice Press in 2021

Library Juice Press
PO Box 188784
Sacramento CA 95818

http://libraryjuicepress.com

This book is printed on acid-free paper

Library of Congress Cataloging-in-Publication Data

Names: Brown, Robin, 1961- author. | Sheidlower, Scott, author.
Title: Seeking to understand : a journey into disability studies and
    libraries / Robin Brown and Scott Sheidlower.
Description: Sacramento, CA : Library Juice Press, 2021. | Includes
    bibliographical references and index. | Summary: "Explores the wide
    range of issues faced by disabled librarians"-- Provided by publisher.
Identifiers: LCCN 2020055478 | ISBN 9781634001069 (paperback ;
    acid-free paper)
Subjects: LCSH: Librarians with disabilities--United States. | Library
    employees with disabilities--United States.
Classification: LCC Z682.4.L46 B76 2021 | DDC 020.92--dc23
LC record available at https://lccn.loc.gov/2020055478

Table of Contents

Acknowledgements

Robin Brown acknowledges the support and encouragement that she has received from her Chief Librarian, Kathleen Dreyer. Thank you to the Personnel and Budget Committee for Professional Assignment Leave. She also acknowledges her husband, Thomas Brown, for companionship, encouragement, and solutions to technical questions.

Scott Sheidlower acknowledges the librarians at York College (CUNY), all of whom have been very supportive; the Professional Staff Congress of CUNY, which has inspired him in its honesty and intelligence; and, of course, his cat, who couldn't care less about this book but because, like all cats, she controls his life and therefore must be acknowledged.

The community that we have worked with to create this book has been very generous. In particular, we appreciate the people who came forward to share narratives with us:

Taiea Anderson
Remy Biggs
Wendy L. Bundy
Kaitlyn Hodges
Katherine Pennavaria
Marisa Reichert
Stephen Weiner

1

Introduction I

Robin Brown

My name is Robin Brown. I work for the A. Philip Randolph Library of the Borough of Manhattan Community College of the City University of New York (CUNY). I was born with cerebral palsy (CP). I am high functioning. I walk with a challenging gait. If you work with me closely, you may eventually see that my hands are mildly affected and that I wear bifocals, which I acquired early because my eyes don't work well together. As I have continued to age with CP, I have developed arthritis, which is complicated by the CP; I have discovered that my life is vastly improved by using a rollator (a walker with wheels). I also suffer from an overwhelming, staggering fatigue. I have an academic appointment, so I am encouraged to do research. I need to publish. That is an important motivation for what became this project. I am very grateful for my College, which has given me reassignment leave to work on this research.

Just over five years ago I went for a walk in Washington Market Park in New York City, which is right next to my College. I have no idea why, but I was feeling very unique, very special, and very alone. This research appeared fully formed in my head. I went back to my office and reached out to Scott Sheidlower from York College (which is another branch of the CUNY system). I'm not sure how well I knew

Scott at that time, but I knew that he had a visible disability. I described my idea and asked if it made any sense. He said, "Of course, and I will help you."

The first payoff, when I posted my idea to a Facebook group for people with CP, was to have another instructional librarian with CP come forward. I was no longer alone. It's been a long road, because both Scott and I have complicated lives. I did another research project in the meantime. We did the Institutional Review Board (IRB) paperwork, which pushed us to develop our first survey. We were wrestling with what platform to use for the survey.

Then Scott sent me the CFP for a special *Library Trends* issue. Our research idea fit right in. I submitted an abstract to the editors and put the first survey up on Google Drive. They accepted it and I started writing. This led to our publishing "Claiming Our Space: A Quantitative and Qualitative Picture of Disabled Librarians" in *Library Trends*.[1] As I took the first dive into the professional literature for this article, I discovered a field that I could spend the rest of my career in. I discovered literature that explained me to myself. This passion for the complexity of this field is one of the founding principles of this book.

One of the things about survey research, particularly if it's been vetted by the IRB, is that you can't change your mind midstream. I read the article "Diversity, Social Justice, and the Future of Libraries," by Morales, Knowles, and Bourg[2] while we were writing the *Library Trends* article. That's why

---

1. Robin Brown and Scott Sheidlower, "Claiming Our Space: A Quantitative and Qualitative Picture of Disabled Librarians," *Library Trends* 67, no. 3 (2019): 471-486.

2. Myrna Morales, Em Claire Knowles, and Chris Bourg, "Diversity, Social Justice, and the Future of Libraries," *Portal: Libraries and the Academy* 14, no. 3 (2014): 439-451.

we went back to the IRB with another phase: we wanted to look at the complexity of identity. We started working on a literature review to support complex identities and, in the process, I began to seek more space. That is the genesis of this book. I want to even out the playing field by bringing issues out of the closet and discussing them. If this makes the life of someone you work with easier, then it's worth it.

One of the life-changing connections that came from doing this work was its deep connection to anti-racism and the critical need to talk about equity, diversity, and inclusion. Do not judge anyone based on surface appearance. This is one of the most important issues raised by this project. This is part of the really important conversation our profession is having about changing the face of libraries to reflect the populations that we are serving. This includes hiring library workers with disabilities. It will be much easier for a library patron with a disability to feel that they are accepted and understood if they have the opportunity to work with someone from the library who also has a disability.[3] There are a whole range of social justice issues that were brought up by the research (see the advocacy chapter). It is our hope, over time, to further engage with social justice issues.

I am no longer alone. In this phase I have met enough librarians with CP to observe that we are all different. I am a research nerd—seeking to understand. This has been an opportunity to exercise my curiosity.

---

3. Jill Lewis, "Information Equality for Individuals with Disabilities: Does It Exist?" *Library Quarterly* 83, no. 3 (2013): 233.

Introduction II

Scott Sheidlower

Robin and I first met while doing committee work for the Library Association of the City University of New York (LACUNY). We both are librarians at CUNY. Robin works at a community college, the Borough of Manhattan Community College, and I work at a senior (four-year) college, York College in Jamaica, Queens. At that time, Robin and I were both on the Library Information Literacy Advisory Committee (LILAC), a CUNY-wide committee that "[creates] information literacy tutorials and assessment tools, providing support to all CUNY librarians by coordinating and running professional development meetings, seminars, and conferences."[1]

I know I was immediately drawn to speaking to Robin as the two of us were the only visibly disabled librarians in the room. We started speaking with one another professionally, about information literacy and the work of LILAC. Eventually, as we walked to the subway (Robin going downtown and I going uptown), we started to speak socially and became friends in addition to colleagues. CUNY also has

---

1. Galina Letnikova, "LILAC: Planted at CUNY Ten Years Ago and Still Blooming" *LACUNY News* 33, no. 2 (2014), https://academicworks.cuny.edu/lg_pubs/46.

a very active librarian's listserv. I always make certain to read anything there that I receive from my friends. Therefore, one day, when I received an email from Robin asking if the "hive mind" thought that disabled librarians were a good topic for research, I immediately responded. I told her that I felt it was a brilliant idea and I wanted to help her work on the topic. I was pleased when she agreed that I could be involved. I also was quite surprised that I had not thought of it on my own. Part of the reason, I think, is that I did not know many disabled librarians. The ones I knew before Robin, Thomas Nielson and Christina Miller, are two very fine librarians and I do not think of either of them as disabled. One of the nice things about librarianship is that it is very accepting of anyone who does the work to get the MLS or the MLIS. I did not include Robin in that list as at that time I had never seen her being a line librarian. This has since changed and I now know three brilliant disabled librarians, besides myself, of course: Christina, Tom, and Robin.

As we write this book, I realize that I have one visible and two invisible disabilities. My left wrist is paralyzed. This means that I have difficulty typing (keyboarding for the Millennial readers). Robin, therefore, is taking the majority of the writing on her shoulders. I can easily do small amounts of typing and so I am doing more editing. Because of this I can easily say that Robin is my teacher in the world of disability studies. My invisible disabilities have less of an effect on my scholarship. One is my epilepsy. Epilepsy does not affect my working on the book. The other disability is osteoarthritis. It affects my walking but not in a major way anymore. This is thanks to a very good orthopedist and physical therapist. I sincerely hope that the reader, whether disabled or not, gets something out of this work that Robin and I have completed.

1. Defining Terms

Berger wrote about disability studies and observed that: "the field can by no means lay claim to a unifying or coherent theoretical approach, as it is constituted by a polyphony if not cacophony of voices. This is to be expected, however, given the interdisciplinary nature of the field and the diversity of phenomena that 'disability' comprises." [1]

The authors surveyed library workers with a wide variety of types of disability. To truly understand the impact of disabilities in libraries, a wide-ranging understanding of the meaning of disability is required. There is expansive literature offering a variety of frames for the phenomena of disability. Because disability is complicated, its causal factors are really difficult to pin down.

Grue offers a useful summary of the different variables that can be considered when discussing disabilities. These factors include politics, economics, psychology, and sociology. [2] Shakespeare balances the two most common models of disability: the medical model and the social model. [3] The medical model defines disability as an individual,

---

1. Ronald J. Berger, *Introducing Disability Studies* (Boulder, CO: Lynne Rienner Publishers, 2013), 25.

2. Jan Grue, "The Social Meaning of Disability: A Reflection on Categorisation, Stigma and Identity," *Sociology of Health & Illness* 38, no. 6 (2016): 958.

3. Tom Shakespeare, *Disability Rights and Wrongs Revisited* (London: Routledge, 2014)

measurable phenomena that needs to be either managed or repaired. Oliver and Barnes label this as the "personal theory."[4] Many disabled people find this model offensive, because it is focused on "individual loss or inability contributing to a dependency model of disability."[5]

The social model views disability as something that is imposed by society. To those who accept the social model, disability isn't about individual weaknesses.[6] Abberly defines this model as one which characterizes "A theory of disability as oppression...[which] emphasizes the social origins of impairment."[7] Advocates of the social model state that that problems of a disabled person are caused by a society which has not created a world that a disabled person can easily maneuver through.

Scotch and Shriner state that disability is simply an expression of the variability that is part of the human condition.[8] They are adamant that challenges for disabled people are caused by external factors that need to adjust to what Pionke calls "functional diversity."[9] Often the social

---

4. Michael Oliver and Colin Barnes, *The New Politics of Disablement* (New York: Palgrave MacMillian, 2012), 32.

5. Len Barton, "Sociology and Disability: Some Emerging Issues," in *Disability and Society: Emerging Issues and Insights,* ed. Len Barton (London: Longman,1996), 8.

6. Barton, 11.

7. Paul Abberley, "The Concept of Oppression and the Development of a Social Theory of Disability." *Disability, Handicap & Society* 2, no. 1 (1987): 17.

8. Richard K. Scotch and Kay Schriner, "Disability as Human Variation: Implications for Policy," *ANNALS of the American Academy of Political and Social Science* 549, no. 1 (1997): 155.

9. Scotch and Schriner, 155; J.J. Pionke, "Beyond ADA Compliance: The

model—as well as its offshoot, the human variation model— leads to a very strong demand for change.

Berg provided a comprehensive summary of the different ways that disability has been framed in law.[10] Making disability a moral problem and a personal failing is mostly a historical issue in the West. However "moral theories continue to influence popular and legal constructions of disability to this day."[11] This refers to the fact that certain challenges are outside the coverage of the Americans with Disabilities Act [ADA] because they are viewed as a matter of personal responsibility.[12] As disability became to be seen as a medical problem, it relieved the individual of moral responsibility.[13] A third frame, which is less well known in most of the United States, looks at the economic impact of disability. Disability is defined as restricting a person's ability to work.[14] The economic model does not fit well with this study, because our respondents are able to work. The final frame offered by Berg is the social/political. As has already been described, the social/political model removes the individual from the equation.[15]

Library as a Place for All," *Urban Library Journal* 23, no. 1 (2017): 1.

10. Paula E. Berg, "Ill/legal: Interrogating the Meaning and Function of the Category of Disability in Anti-discrimination Law," *Yale Law & Policy Review,* 18 (1999): 1.

11. Berg, 6.

12. Berg, 11.

13. Berg, 6

14. Berg, 8.

15. Berg, 9.

Cameron discusses a less well-known affirmation model.[16] First offered by Swain and French, the affirmation model suggests that being disabled can be a positive experience.[17] Cameron asserts that a disability can be "valuable, exciting, interesting and intrinsically satisfying."[18] Cameron makes it clear that the affirmation model is an extension of the social model.[19] The affirmation model is a direct challenge to the "tragedy model [see above]."[20]

Chronic Illness as a Form of Disability

The disability rights movement rejects the pairing of illness with disability.[21] Illness, to the advocates for the social model, represents a need for medical support, and is an individual problem.[22] Wendell stresses that some disabled people have physical challenges that are not connected with ableist social structures.[23] There are many people who choose to identify

---

16. Colin Cameron, "Further Towards an Affirmation Model," in *Disability Studies: Emerging Insights and Perspectives*, ed. Thomas Campbell (Leeds, UK: Disability Press, 2008), 14-30.

17. John Swain and Sally French, "Towards an Affirmation Model of Disability," *Disability & Society* 15, no. 4 (2000): 569-582.

18. Cameron, "Further Towards," 20.

19. Cameron, 27.

20. Swain and French, "Towards," 572.

21. Susan Wendell, "Unhealthy Disabled: Treating Chronic Illnesses as Disabilities," *Hypatia* 16, no. 4 (2001): 17.

22. Wendell, 17-18.

23. Wendell, 18.

with the disabled community who have been impaired by chronic illness.[24] This is a reflection of the fact that "chronic illness is an increasing phenomena, and consequently one that must impact the workforce."[25]

Aging and Disablement

Just as disability is not necessarily caused by an illness, aging can bring about disability, but does not necessarily do so. It's a complicated issue, because aging also complicates disability. The aging of the population is also a factor in the increasing numbers of people who self-identify as being disabled.[26] Bickenbach, et al. conflated aging and disability; they observed that the needs of two populations are so similar, that they should be viewed together.[27]

---

24. Margaret Vickers, *Work and Unseen Chronic illness: Silent Voices*, (New York: Routledge, 2002); Wendell, 20.

25. Vickers, 12.

26. Colin Barnes, "Disability, the Organization of Work, and the Need for Change," statement presented to the Organisation for Economic Co-operation and Development Conference "Transforming Disability Into Ability," March 6, 2003, 2; "Persons with a Disability: Labor Force Characteristics—2018," *Economic News Release: Persons with a Disability: Labor Force Characteristics*, US Department of Labor, Bureau of Labor Statistics, February 26, 2019.

27. Jerome Bickenbach, et al., "The Toronto Declaration on Bridging Knowledge, Policy and Practice in Aging and Disability: Toronto, Canada, March 30, 2012," *International Journal of Integrated Care* 12 (2012): 1; Joseph P. Shapiro, *No Pity: People with Disabilities Forging a New Civil Rights Movement.* (New York: Three Rivers Press, 1994), 6.

Discussion

This topic is very complicated. Any attempt to define disability as not being able to work, is contradicted by this study (see chapter 4 for further discussion of this point.) Some consideration of the medical model makes sense because for some people, medical support can be helpful.

For the purposes of this book we chose a middle ground. Generally, there is a physiological issue, but stress created by infrastructure could be set right if it mattered enough to society. Disability is not completely social and can be affected by physiology.[28] This is similar to the definition offered by the World Health Organization (WHO):

> Disability [is] an umbrella term for impairments, activity limitations, and participation restrictions. Disability refers to the negative aspects of the interaction between individuals with a health condition (such as cerebral palsy, Down syndrome, depression) and personal and environmental factors (such as negative attitudes, inaccessible transportation and public buildings, and limited social supports).[29]

The authors found that chronic illness can be an impairment and needs accommodation in the context of library work. There is a difference between a chronic illness and a common cold. Impairments come from illnesses that create long-term disabling conditions. There are a lot of commonalities. Likewise, we had respondents who were struggling with disabilities brought on by illness and aging. Within the context of workforce development and

---

28. Adrienne Asch, "Critical Race Theory, Feminism, and Disability: Reflections on Social Justice and Personal Identity," *Ohio State Law Journal* 62 (2001): 410.

29. World Health Organization, "World Report on Disability: Summary," 7

accommodation, the needs of those suffering from chronic illness, the impacts of aging, or impairments are very similar. We encourage our readers to keep open minds about how disability is defined.

2. A Deeper Dive into Disabilities Studies

The social critiques that come out of disabilities studies are worth considering.

Individualism and Capitalism: A Critique

"Ideals of community care can be used to create inclusive work environments and beat back against the tide of toxic individualism epitomized by ideologies of whiteness and capitalism."[1]

What makes individualism so toxic? Our culture is structured around individual achievement.[2] "[In capitalism] the rhetoric and incentives rewarding workaholic behavior" make it difficult for people to succeed if they have family demands or require care themselves.[3] Oliver and Barnes identify individualism as "the core ideology of capitalism."[4]

There is in the disability studies literature a critique of capitalism. Many issues that come up when considering the conditions of the disabled are fundamental critiques of how our society and culture have evolved. This is not a new idea.

---

1. Jessica Schomberg, "Disability at Work: Libraries, Built to Exclude," in *The Politics and Theory of Critical Librarianship*, ed. Karen P. Nicholson and Maura Seale (Sacramento, CA: Library Juice Press, 2018), 120.

2. Schomberg, "Disability at Work," 118.

3. Schomberg, "Disability at Work," 119.

4. Oliver and Barnes, 119.

Russell quotes Helen Keller, addressing the "Women's Peace Party" in 1916, identifying herself as a "socialist."[5]

Oliver and Barnes also make a coherent argument regarding the impact of capitalism on the lives of persons with disabilities. They cover in great detail the argument that current economic models of disability arrived with the Industrial Revolution.[6] This is also covered by McRuer, including the ideas of efficiency studies, and scientific management.[7] Russell points out the sheer inhumanity of the capitalist system.[8]

Individualism also touches on one of the classic definitions of disability, i.e. that "disability is an individual problem."[9] This is important. It means that whatever stresses or adjustments that are required by impairment, it is the responsibility of the individual or of the individual's family.

Shakespeare argues interdependence is inevitable, and personal independence is an illusion.[10] The "dependency" model of disability is often critiqued. The dependency model is an outgrowth of the medical model, stressing "individual loss or inabilities."[11] The social call for independence is a facet

5. Marta Russell, *Beyond Ramps: Disability at the End of the Social Contract: A Warning from an Uppity Crip* (Monroe, ME: Common Courage Press, 1998), 57.

6. Oliver and Barnes, 55

7. McRuer, "Crip Theory," 88-89.

8. Russell, 68.

9. Michael Oliver and Colin Barnes, *The New Politics of Disablement,* (New York: Palgrave Macmillan, 2012), 3.

10. Tom Shakespeare, *Help: Imagining Welfare.* (Birmingham, UK: Venture Press, 2000), 78-79.

11. Barton, "Sociology and Disability," 8.

of ableism. The authors disagree and believe that it is good to depend upon each other.

As Oliver noted: "No one in a modern industrial society is completely independent, for we live in a state of mutual interdependence. The dependence of disabled people, therefore, is not a feature which marks them out as different in kind from the rest of the population but as different in degree."[12]

Normal

Disabilities studies scholars often wrestle with the idea of normal. Oliver and Barnes write that "normal" sets up a binary system, enforcing an either/or situation.[13] Davis describes the evolution of the idea of average or normal out of the development of statistical science in the nineteenth century. The development of statistical science stressed "the concept of a norm, particularly a normal body."[14]

Jenny Morris writes about why normality is so troublesome: "the idea of normality is inherently tied up with ideas about what is right, what is desirable and what belongs."[15] People with disabilities challenge normality because they are different (regardless of whether it is visible) and they have different needs.[16]

---

12. Mike Oliver, "Social Policy and Disability: The Creation of Dependency," *Tidskrift För Rättssociologi*, 5, no.1 (1988): 31-32.

13. Oliver and Barnes, 89

14. Lennard J. Davis, *Enforcing Normalcy: Disability, Deafness, and the Body*, (New York: Verso, 1995), 31.

15. Jenny Morris, *Pride*, 16.

16. Morris, 18.

Susan Wendell writes critically of "the disciplines of normality."[17] This is another way of expressing the stigma that is associated with being different and is clearly associated with both external stigma and internalized stigma (see chapter 4 on Work and Disability).

Normal becomes even more suspect, if we consider what it really means. "'Normal' is an artificial construct built upon the white, middle-class, male, nondisabled bodymind."[18] This is connected to pushing back on the idea of normal to be both an act of feminism, but also of anti-racism (see chapter 8 on Race).

17. Susan Wendell, *The Rejected Body*, (New York: Routledge, 1986), 88.

18. Corbett Joan O Toole, *Fading Scars: My Queer Disability History*, 2nd ed. (Berkeley, CA: Reclamation Press, 2019), 7.

3. DISABILITY RIGHTS MOVEMENT

The history of disabilities has already been referred to. Disabled people were removed from the economy with the arrival of the Industrial Revolution. Social Darwinism and statistical science created a normal or average paradigm that classified the disabled as sick, dependent, and in need of repair. Like many civil rights movements, the back story is important to remind everyone of what the situation used to be like. The medical, pitiful, dependent model is often demonstrated by the "poster child" fundraising strategy.[1] "Rejected is society's deeply held thinking of tin cups and Tiny Tim—the idea that disabled people are childlike, dependent, and in need of charity or pity."[2]

The first phase of the battle for civil rights for the disabled has been traced by the filmmakers James Lebrecht and Nicole Newnham to a unique camp for disabled teenagers in upstate New York, where the disabled were treated equally. The alumni of Camp Jenna worked together to pull off the first round of civil rights protests.[3]

---

1. Joseph P. Shapiro. *No Pity: People with Disabilities Forging a New Civil Rights Movement.* (New York: Three Rivers Press, 1994), 13.

2. Shapiro, 14.

3. *Crip Camp: A Disability Revolution*, directed by James Lebrecht and Nicole Newnham (Hollywood, CA: Higher Ground Productions, 2020).

The battle for civil rights for the disabled entered a new phase with student activists at the University of California, Berkeley. "The disability rights movement was born the day [Ed] Roberts arrived on the Berkeley campus."[4] The civil rights movement, the women's movement, and the fight for rights for the profoundly disabled, all developed simultaneously.[5] Many of the social and technological innovations that the mobility challenged now depend on sprang out of the needs of the community of disabled students at Berkeley.[6] Although programs for disabled students began to spring up at other universities, very few "incorporate[d] the self-help approach of the Berkeley students."[7]

Also coming out of Berkeley was the 504 Sit-In at the Federal Office Building in San Francisco. Members of the disabled community and their allies took over the Federal Office Building in San Francisco for twenty-eight days in April of 1977, to force the HEW Secretary Frank Califano to sign regulations to enforce section 504 of the Rehabilitation Act of 1973.[8] The challenge concerned how to implement the following paragraph from the statute:

> No otherwise qualified individual with a disability in the United States, as defined in section 705 (20) of this title, shall,

---

4. Shapiro, 41.

5. Shapiro, 47.

6. Shapiro, 51.

7. Shapiro, 53.

8. OToole. *Fading Scars,* 28-47.; Andrew Grim, "Sitting-in for Disability Rights: The Section 504 Protests of the 1970s," O Say Can You See: Stories from the Museum, National Museum of American History, July 8, 2015, https://americanhistory.si.edu/blog/sitting-disability-rights-section-504-protests-1970s.

solely by reason of his or her disability, be excluded from the participation in, be denied the benefits of, or be subjected to discrimination under any program or activity receiving Federal financial assistance or under any program or activity conducted by any Executive agency or by the United States Postal Service.[9]

What the demonstrators wanted was for there to be regulations enacted to put this into effect. They wanted the regulations to not dilute the power of the statute.

When looking at the connection between anti-racism and disabled civil rights, it must be acknowledged that the 504 Sit-In was made possible by the fact that the Black Panther Party of Oakland, CA stepped up to feed the demonstrators on a daily basis for the length of the sit-in.[10]

The sense of the rights of people with disabilities to manage their own lives came out of what became known as the 504 Movement and the language that was included in the Rehabilitation Act of 1973. This also sparked an independent living movement, which stressed that even those who needed help with basic needs should be able to control their own lives.[11]

There was another benchmark that changed the expectations of the disabled. The Individuals with Disabilities Education Act (1975) gave disabled children access to

9. US Department of Labor, Office of the Assistant Secretary for Administration and Management. *Section 504, Rehabilitation Act of 1973*, accessed February 24, 2020, https://www.dol.gov/agencies/oasam/centers-offices/civil-rights-center/statutes/section-504-rehabilitation-act-of-1973.

10. OToole, 90.

11. OToole, 48-77.

public education.[12] Activists with disabilities have used state legislation, the media, and the courts to demand equal treatment, often moving one case forward at a time.

All of this was the heritage of the Americans with Disabilities Act of 1995, in two ways. The ADA built on the legislation that had come before it.[13] At the same time, the expectations of the disabled, and the habit of activism that had been building since the 1970s, helped push it through Congress.[14] This habit of activism is a notable resource. At stake is allowing people with disabilities to participate equally, regardless of whether it is school, shopping, dining, the movies, or work.

Discussion

The need to not be excluded is often an individual journey that starts with confronting a personal experience and deciding one has had enough. Disability history is often the story of such individuals going public with their demands and moving everyone forward with their hard work. This reminds us of the feminist statement "the personal is political."[15] Our personal experiences are relevant, because they may say something about what is possible for others like us.

---

12. Kim E. Nielsen, *A Disability History of the United States*, (Boston: Beacon Press, 2012), 167.

13. Nielsen, "A Disability History," 180.

14. The Minnesota Governor's Council on Developmental Disabilities, "The ADA Legacy Project: Moments in Disability History 27," The Minnesota Governor's Council on Developmental Disabilities, 2020, https://mn.gov/mnddc/ada-legacy/ada-legacy-moment27.html.

15. Hanish.

4. Work and Disability

As noted in the introduction, this book surveys library workers who self-identify as disabled. Although Vernon's work is intersectional (dealing with disabled women of color) it is worth noting what she says about employment and its importance to disabled people: "Employment is the means to life. It enables our physical survival as well as being a key determinant of our sense of mental well-being...this is no different for disabled people."[1]

When using to the economic model of disability, many authors refer to the connection between disability and the ability to work. Disability has been defined as an inability to work.[2] Being able to participate in the workforce makes someone part of society.[3] Nancy Mairs juxtaposes "social value" and "economic productivity."[4]

---

1. Ayesha Vernon, "A Stranger in Many Camps: The Experience of Disabled Black and Ethnic Minority Women," in *Encounters with Strangers: Feminism and Disability*, ed. Jenny Morris (London: Women's Press, 1996), 53.

2. Kim Nielsen, "Helen Keller and the Politics of Civic Fitness," in *The New Disability History: American Perspectives,* ed. Paul K. Longmore and Lauri Umansky (New York: NYU Press, 2001), 271; Colin Barnes, "Disability, the Organization of Work."

3. Paul Abberley, "Work, Utopia, and Impairment." in *Disability and Society: Emerging Issues and Insights,* ed. Len Barton (London: Longman, 1996), 61; David M. Engel and Frank W. Munger, *Rights of Inclusion: Law and Identity in the Life Stories of Americans with Disabilities* (Chicago: University of Chicago Press, 2003), 114.

4. Nancy Mairs, "Sex and Death and the Crippled Body: A Meditation" in

Oliver and Barnes speak of the appearance of disability as a cultural phenomenon concurrent with the Industrial Revolution, with the appearance of "individualized wage labor of the factory."[5] This confirms the cultural connection between disability and the ability to work.

Noel writes in support of the value of including people with disabilities in the workforce.[6] Among other things, she confirms the productivity and reliability of the disabled workforce,[7] which is also confirmed by our research (see Data Discussion). Our research also confirms the need to "[rethink] current job descriptions."[8] Dow et al. did an interesting linguistic study of job ads, calling for the elimination of library jargon in order to make ads clearer for applicants on the autistic spectrum[9] (see Advocacy).

There are multiple challenges faced by the working disabled. Wilson-Kovacs, et al. describe a "glass cliff" being faced by leaders who are "members of marginalized groups."[10]

Disability Studies: Enabling the Humanities, ed. Sharon L. Snyder, Brenda Jo Brueggemann, and Rosemarie Garland Thomson (New York: Modern Language Association of America, 2002), 168.

5. Oliver and Barnes, *The New Politics,* 16.

6. Rita Thomas Noel, "Employing the Disabled: A How and Why Approach," *Training & Development Journal* 44, no. 8 (1990): 26-32.

7. Noel, 30.

8. Noel, 30.

9. Mirah Jane Dow, Brady D. Lund, and William K. Douthit, "Investigating the Link between Unemployment and Disability," *International Journal of Information, Diversity, & Inclusion (IJIDI)* 4, no. 1 (2020).

10. Dana Wilson-Kovacs, et al. "'Just Because You Can Get a Wheelchair in the Building Doesn't Necessarily Mean That You Can Still Participate': Barriers to the Career Advancement of Disabled Professionals," *Disability &*

They indicate that leadership positions can be "precarious and associated with a greater risk of failure."[11] Wilson-Kovacs, et al. describe how the experiences of disabled managers both parallel and diverge from the experiences of managers from other marginalized groups.[12]

As Schriner reports, the employment statistics for people with disabilities are consistently lower than those for the able-bodied.[13] There is a persistent international link between poverty and disability."[14] Schriner also advocates for society-wide transformation. "Transformative rehabilitation practice" seeks "inclusive community and economic development [and] political action."[15] In a similar tone, Shklar's analysis concludes with a call for "providing opportunities for work to earn a living wage for all who need it or demand it."[16] Shklar is writing from the perspective of having a deep concern for racial justice, and probably did not consider the implications of her call for those who have a disability.

Society 23, no. 7 (2008): 705.

11. Wilson-Kovacs, et al., 707.

12. Wilson-Kovacs, et al., 709-711.

13. Kay Schriner, "A Disability Studies Perspective on Employment Issues and Policies for Disabled People: An International View," in *Handbook of Disability Studies*, ed. by Gary L. Albrecht, Katherine D. Seelman, and Michael Bury (Thousand Oaks, CA: Sage Publications, 2001), 645.

14. Alan Roulstone, "Disabled People, Work and Employment: A Global Perspective," in *Routledge Handbook of Disability Studies*, ed. by Nick Watson, Carol Thomas, and Alan Roulstone (New York: Routledge, 2013), 211.

15. Schriner, 654.

16. Judith N. Shklar, *American Citizenship: The Quest for Inclusion,* (Cambridge, MA: Harvard University Press, 1995), 99.

The Impact of the ADA

Vornholt, et al. found that the Americans with Disabilities Act (ADA) has not improved the employment prospects for disabled workers. This is apparently due to perceptions of stigma and misplaced concern about the cost of accommodations.[17] The definition of disability, and thus eligibility to be protected under the ADA, is subtle and difficult to fulfill.[18] Tucker provides a useful analysis of how various facets of the ADA have evolved and have been implemented.[19] Often the judicial challenges have been an exercise in frustration: "The courts either do not understand, or do not accept, the concept of reasonable accommodations as a necessary component of the civil rights premise underlying the ADA."[20] Nevertheless, there have been some important social changes, raising awareness and expectations.[21] Within the context of education, the ADA "is important because it both defines who a disabled student is and sets up the relationship between the disabled student and the faculty member."[22]

---

17. Katharina Vornholt, et al., "Disability and Employment–Overview and Highlights," *European Journal of Work and Organizational Psychology* 27, no. 1 (2018): 45.

18. Berg, "Ill/legal: Interrogating."

19   Bonnie Poitras Tucker, "The ADA's Revolving Door: Inherent Flaws in the Civil Rights Paradigm," *Ohio State Law Journal* 62 (2001): 335-389.

20. Tucker, 353.

21. Tucker, 383-384.

22. Mark Aaron Polger and Scott Sheidlower, *Engaging Diverse Learners: Teaching Strategies for Academic Librarians.* (Santa Barbara, CA: Libraries Unlimited, 2017), 27.

Thomas and Gostin update our understanding of the importance of the ADA by stressing the importance of the ADA Amendments Act (2008).[23] They also stress the importance of access to employment in order to provide access to health care.[24] Access to health insurance if you are unemployed is easier since Obamacare was implemented.

Carpenter did a survey exploring how widely accommodations are offered by college and university libraries in Ohio. Several issues were identified as impacting the availability of accommodations: "public versus private institutions; whether the library was constructed before or after the ADA was enacted; the extent to which physical facilities exacerbate accessibility issues; and whether there are any disabled library staff."[25]

Particularly in the context of the ADA, and framing disability rights as a civil rights struggle, there is one major difference between the disabled and other who struggle for civil rights. In order to be protected by the ADA, a person with a disability must prove their disability.[26]

---

23. Victoria L. Thomas and Lawrence O. Gostin, "The Americans with Disabilities Act: Shattered Aspirations and New Hope," *JAMA* 301, no. 1 (2009): 95-97.

24. Thomas and Gostin, 96.

25. Scott Carpenter, "The Americans with Disabilities Act: Accommodation in Ohio," *College and Research Libraries* 57 no. 6 (1996): 558.

26. Ruth O'Brien, *Crippled Justice: The History of Modern Disability Policy in the Workplace.* (Chicago: University of Chicago Press, 2001): 14-15.

Passing and Stigma

Work and disabilities studies relate to issues about disclosure.[27] For some disabled people, disclosure is not a choice. For others, it's an ongoing conversation related to passing. What is passing? It is an attempt to join the mainstream, to appear to not be an outlier. To pass is to acknowledge that the other is a stigmatic identity. To be constantly monitoring your identity can be exhausting. There is literature from disability studies that describes what it is like to hide that you are part of the other: "You are like everyone else, but only as long as you hide or minimize your disability. Both passing and overcoming take their toll."[28] Passing and overcoming are products of the medical model of disability: disability is wrong and it needs to be fixed.

Brune and Wilson realized that when we recognize ourselves as other, the broader discussion about civil rights becomes deeply meaningful. Multiple identities "interact and affect one another."[29] They also remind us that passing is very much about a false dichotomy. Life is not about being either disabled or normal.[30]

Martinez, et al. report on research with transgender employees, using the term "authenticity."[31] They are

27. Jans, et.al., "Getting Hired"

28. Simi Linton, *Claiming Disability: Knowledge and Identity,* (New York: NYU Press, 1998), 54.

29. Brune and Wilson, "Disability and Passing," 2.

30. Brune and Wilson, "Disability and Passing," 2.

31. Larry R. Martinez, et al., "The Importance Of Being 'Me': The Relation Between Authentic Identity Expression And Transgender Employees' Work-related Attitudes And Experiences," *Journal of Applied Psychology* 102, no. 2 (2017): 215-226.

exploring "authentic identity expression," [32] meaning that an individual's public persona matches their internal sense of self. The courage that it takes to be publicly authentic also relates to internal self-acceptance. The personal need for public authenticity stands against any sense of stigmatization. The need to pass is very much connected with stigma, whether it is internal or external.

The theories that undergird disabilities studies have tremendous explanatory power. That means that they show us what's going on. One of the most disturbing frames is something that was first described in a different generation and at a very different time. Goffman's "Stigma: Notes on the Management of Spoiled Identity" was originally published in 1963.[33] It continues to be cited by many different authors. Stigma is defined by Goffman as "the situation of the individual who is disqualified from full social acceptance."[34] All of the identities being considered in this study touch on issues of social acceptance.

A more detailed definition of stigma was offered by Link and Phelan: "Stigma exists when elements of labeling, stereotyping, separation, status loss, and discrimination occur together in a power situation that allows them."[35] This act of categorizing someone is inevitably based on "first

---

32. Martinez, et al., 215.

33. Erving Goffman, *Stigma: Notes on the Management of Spoiled* Identity (New York: Simon and Schuster, 1963).

34. Goffman, Preface.

35. Bruce G. Link and Jo C. Phelan, "Conceptualizing Stigma," *Annual Review of Sociology* 27, no. 1 (2001): 377.

appearances…[making] certain assumptions about what the individual before us ought to be."[36]

Scambler and Hopkins differentiate between "enacted and felt stigma."[37] Enacted stigma is discrimination coming from the outside. Felt stigma is closely connected with shame. Shame arrives when the social standards of what a person ought to be are internalized. We internalize social standards and "agree that [we do] indeed fall short of what [we] really ought to be."[38]

Jans, et al. documented the truly pervasive influence of stigma in the lives of working people with disabilities, particularly in influencing the decision of whether or not to disclose disability.[39] Similar conclusions were reached by Vornholt, et al. regarding the employment prospects of people with mental illness. Stigma is a very important issue when looking at employment.[40]

Invisible Disabilities

Invisible disabilities map very closely with the issues of stigma and passing. For a person with an invisible disability who needs some form of reasonable accommodation, there is often a concern about stigma as a consequence of self-identification.

---

36. Goffman, *Stigma*, 2.

37. Graham Scambler and Anthony Hopkins, "Being Epileptic: Coming to Terms with Stigma," *Sociology of Health & Illness* 8, no. 1 (1986): 33.

38. Goffman, *Stigma*, 7.

39. Jans, et al., "Getting Hired," 158.

40. Katharina Vornholt, et al. "Disability and Employment – Overview and Highlights." *European Journal of Work and Organizational Psychology* 27, no. 1 (2018): 40-55.

"The focus on information management is shaped not only by the threat of stigmatization but also by concerns of authenticity and legitimacy."[41]

Davis summarizes the issues that beset persons with invisible disabilities. "When individuals are not 'seen' as disabled, it can be more difficult for them to secure the assistance or accommodation they need to function effectively."[42] This is confirmed by Cook and Clement, and connects to what Kattari, Olzman, and Hanna describe as the "policing of bodies."[43] This refers to judging persons using public accommodations, if they are not clearly disabled.

Valeras points out that people with invisible disabilities challenge the binary thinking of disabled versus able bodied.[44] As the authors continue their research among people who accept the disabled label, yet are highly functioning, they agree that disability and able-bodied is not a dyad, but rather fall on a continuum.

Cook and Clement provide an excellent overview of the challenges of managing people with invisible disabilities: "it is important to consider ways in which you can accommodate

41. Judith A. Clair, Joy E. Beatty, and Tammy L. MacLean, "Out of Sight but Not Out of Mind: Managing Invisible Social Identities in the Workplace," *Academy of Management Review* 30, no. 1 (2005): 79.

42. N. Ann Davis, "Invisible Disability," *Ethics* 116, no. 1 (2005): 157.

43. Samantha Cook and Kristina Clement, "Navigating the Hidden Void: The Unique Challenges of Accommodating Library Employees with Invisible Disabilities," *Journal of Academic Librarianship* 45, no. 5 (2019); Shanna K. Kattari, Miranda Olzman, and Michele D. Hanna, "'You Look Fine!' Ableist Experiences by People with Invisible Disabilities," *Affilia* 3, no. 4 (2018): 481.

44. Aimee Valeras, "'We Don't Have a Box': Understanding Hidden Disability Identity Utilizing Narrative Research Methodology," *Disability Studies Quarterly* 30, no. 3/4 (2010).

people with invisible disabilities without drawing unnecessary attention."[45]

Vickers wrote extensively on chronic illness as an invisible disability. In particular, Vickers mentions the international symbol for the disabled, which creates an assumption that all disabilities are visible:

> The expectation, especially by those who are not disabled, that all disabled people are wheelchair users, tends to be underscored by the use of the universal disability symbol (which depicts a person seated in a wheelchair) which is radically used to designate, for example disabled parking or disabled toilet facilities...However, such depictions may present problems for people with invisible disability when they legitimately make use of such facilities.[46]

The impact of invisible disabilities on librarianship should be part of an examination of stresses on library worker's identities.[47] People with a range of invisible disabilities have found a home in libraries.[48]

---

45. Cook and Clement, "Navigating," 2.

46. Vickers, *Work*, 7

47. Mary E. Brown, "Invisible Debility: Attitudes toward the Under-represented in Library Workplaces," *Public Library Quarterly* 34, no. 2 (2015): 124-133.

48. Robin Brown and Scott Sheidlower. "Claiming Our Space: A Quantitative and Qualitative Picture of Disabled Librarians," *Library Trends* 67, no. 3 (2019): 471-486.

5. Work, Passing, Stigma, and Invisibility (Discussion)

This study is part of the literature that pushes back against assumptions that disabled people are unable to work.[1] This is a very important trend in disabilities studies literature. By actively describing factors in the working life of disabled library workers, it is our hope to shift the perception about functional variations and increase the likelihood that disabled applicants will be considered. Remember that disability and able-bodied are not a dyad, but rather a continuum. When we talk about functional variation, the variations cover a truly wide range of impairment. This is why it is impossible to make any assumptions about job applicants or colleagues who demonstrate differences.

As we ponder what that really means, the transformative work that is described by Schriner and Shklar give us a road map to take seriously and goals to reach for.[2] This research has led to the realization that political action is radically

---

1. Vickers, *Work and Unseen Chronic Illness*; Lita H. Jans, H. Stephen Kaye, and Erica C. Jones, "Getting Hired: Successfully Employed People with Disabilities Offer Advice on Disclosure, Interviewing, and Job Search," *Journal of Occupational Rehabilitation* 22, no. 2 (2012): 155-165; Paul Harpur, "Naming, Blaming and Claiming Ableism: The Lived Experiences of Lawyers and Advocates with Disabilities," *Disability & Society* 29, no. 8 (2014): 1234-1247.

2. Schriner, "A Disabilities Studies Perspective," 645. Shklar, *American Citizenship,* 99.

important in 2020 when the basic assumptions of our society are in play in a national election. The implications of our research for widespread change are further explored in the Advocacy chapter.

The dive into the literature on the ADA was very sobering. It was startling to discover how difficult it is to be successful when suing someone on the basis of the ADA. There is some evidence, at least in higher education, that the ADA, although cumbersome, has created an atmosphere of awareness and change. The impact of the disabled on higher education will be further considered under Inclusive Education.

Passing and Stigma

Passing, meaning being seen as something someone is not, enters the conversation as we think more broadly about the types and severity of impairments. This is one of the founding questions of our research, because we both understand what it means to pass:

> **Robin Brown:** The time was fifteen years ago. I was working for Rutgers University, Newark at the time, walking out of Newark Penn Station, up Raymond Boulevard to campus. I was on my way home. I remember the street corner. I'm on the ground, having just tripped over a crack in the sidewalk. I called a friend, absolutely hysterical. The problem wasn't a skinned knee and bruises. The problem was that I was in denial about my disability, and my bubble had been burst. The journey toward self-acceptance has been about growing in my understanding of my unique and interesting body. Most days dressing so that my brace is obvious. My life has been enriched by claiming my space as a disabled librarian.[3]

---

3. Robin Brown, "Passing," The Adventures of a Three Wheeled Librarian, March 20, 2018, http://threewheeledlibrarian.weebly.com/adventures-of-a-three-wheeled-librarian/passing2842796.

Scott Sheidlower: During the 1970s, when I was going for my bachelor's degree at Hunter College of the City University of New York (CUNY), during one of my classes we were having a discussion about something related to ourselves. I said, during the discussion something along the lines of, "Blah, blah, blah, because of my disability." The discussion stopped and everyone in the class, I would guess around fifteen or twenty people stared at me. One of my fellow classmates said, "You're disabled?" They were genuinely surprised. I realized that the class, and indeed most people I knew then weren't aware that I have a paralyzed left wrist which affects my ability to move and use my left hand. At that time, I always carried a book or a newspaper in my left hand in such a way that my wrist was camouflaged. Of course, my epilepsy is a hidden disability. I make certain that I now hold my hand in such a way that my disability is very visible. From the 1970s to the 2000s, over thirty years, both society and I have changed and I am proud of being disabled.[4]

Confronting the connection between passing, shame, and stigma changes everything. Even if passing were possible, it is connected to internalized ableism. Can those of us who identify as people with disabilities push back against any symptoms of shame? Can we inventory our relationship with ourselves and root out internalized ableism? Shame is something that needs to be struggled against. A strong sense of being different brings a self-consciousness that is exhausting.[5] The ongoing need to be negotiating life when you are aware that you do not fit in is really hard work. This is a factor in the overwhelming fatigue that has been documented by research.

---

4. Scott Sheidlower, "Love, Sex, Disability, Coming Out and John Travolta in New York and Jerusalem: A Twenty-Year Journey," *Graduate Journal of Social Science* 12, no. 1 (2016): 118.

5. Goffman, *Stigma*, 14.

Studying the literature on passing also brings up the issue of individual authenticity. It is worthwhile for thoughtful people, in honor of the people who have really struggled with painful issues, to consider what it means to lead an authentic life.

Invisible Disabilities

The number of people who came forward to participate in our work who identify as having invisible disabilities was larger than the authors expected. This stresses the importance of understanding the range of impairments that are possible. This led to an important insight for anyone who uses accommodations on mass transit. We suggest that it's important to stop judging people who are riding elevators or sitting in the "disabled" seat on the train. This comes back to the idea of "policing bodies." [6]

It's worth noting how difficult it is for people with invisible disabilities to get accommodations at work. Invisible disabilities are very common and cannot always be easily identified by others. Further work needs to be done to give co-workers the space to privately self-identify and get their needs met. Our research documented that the choice to self-identify for reasons of accommodation can lead to publicizing a previously hidden disability, which can lead then to problems with stigma. Perhaps we need to talk more about respecting people's privacy.

When meditating on both visible and invisible disabilities, an issue appeared that is deeply connected with equity, diversity, and inclusion. All of us should consider carefully what assumptions we are making when we meet new people.

---

6. Katter et al., "You Look Fine!," 481.

This touches on issues of appearance. This is further considered when exploring the connection between disabilities activism and anti-racism. This was one of the truly useful outcomes of this research.

6. DISABILITIES AND QUEER STUDIES

Robert McRuer offers an extended analysis of the intersection between queer theory and disability theory.[1] Since nobody meets the normative standards all the time, McRuer observed that "We are all disabled/queer."[2] There are significant connections between these two fields. Corbett draws important parallels between the disabled and the queer. She makes a convincing case looking at the pressure to "pass," the idea of "normalization," and the contrast between "stigma and pride."[3] "These are social problems for all of us who are outside the norm."[4]

Davis also draws a connection between disability studies and queer theory, suggesting "clear parallels between people's insistence on being told how someone 'knows' that they are 'really' gay and their insistence on being provided with some proof that they are really disabled."[5] Is it possible to tell if someone is gay? Schwartz and Kemping discussed what is

---

1. Robert McRuer, *Crip Theory: Cultural Signs of Queerness and Disability* (New York: NYU Press, 2006).

2. McRuer, *Crip Theory*, 57.

3. Jenny Corbett, "A Proud Label: Exploring the Relationship Between Disability Politics and Gay Pride," *Disability & Society* 9, no. 3 (1994): 343-357.

4. Corbett, "Proud Label," 348.

5. N. Ann Davis, "Invisible Disability," *Ethics* 116, no. 1 (2005): 207.

popularly called "gaydar," the idea that it is possible to spot a gay person.[6] "Gaydar works sometimes but not all the time."[7]

Exile and Pride is a memoir that looks at the intersection of disability and queer studies.[8] Clare makes the following important point about disabled workers in general: "to believe that achievement contradicts disability is to pair helplessness with disability, a pairing for which crips pay an awful price."[9]

The painful story of Sharon Kowalski is often cited as a collision between disability rights and queer studies.[10] Ms. Kowalski was living with Karen Thompson as a "closeted couple" in 1983, when she became disabled in a car accident. Her parents refused to recognize their relationship, not granting Ms. Kowalski's desire to go home from the nursing home (where her parents had placed her) to live with her partner. The legal wrangling continued until 1991, when the Minnesota State District Court gave Ms. Thompson guardianship of Ms. Kowalski, recognizing them as a family.[11]

---

6. Pepper Schwartz and Martha Kempner, "Orientation and Identity" in *50 Great Myths of Human Sexuality* (Chichester, UK: John Wiley & Sons, 2015), 41-44.

7. Schwartz and Kempner, "Orientation and Identity," 43.

8. Eli Clare, *Exile and Pride: Disability, Queerness, and Liberation* (Durham, NC: Duke University Press, 2015).

9. Clare, *Exile and Pride*, 9; "Crips" is a term sometimes used by the disabled about themselves. It is a shortened form of the word cripple. Used by the non-disabled, it is considered derogatory.

10. Yvon Appleby, "Out in the Margins," *Disability & Society* 9, no. 1 (1994): 21; McRuer, *Crip Theory*, 81-102.

11. Tamar Lewin, "Disabled Woman's Care Given to Lesbian Partner," *New York Times*, December 18, 1991.

Multiple identities intersect in Appleby's narrative. These multiple identities are found in the stresses that are reported by disabled lesbians when interacting with able-bodied lesbians, struggling to find a level of acceptance, in a community that promotes strength and independence.[12] This also comes up at the intersection of feminism and disability.

Queer Studies and Libraries

There is a literature that describes the experience of gay people within librarianship. The personal narratives therein reflect many different kinds of libraries. The general theme is finding acceptance within libraries, and finding an ability to serve the LGBTQ community.[13] One of the important themes is that "LGBT people are no different than everyone else."[14] It is also necessary here to acknowledge Barbara Gittings, who was a founder of the gay rights movement, and a gifted librarian.[15]

Discussion

The authors find that disabilities studies and queer studies really connect with the issue of normality. How do we define how human beings ought to be? This could be connected

---

12. Appleby, "Out," 22-25.

13. Tracy Nectoux, ed., *Out Behind the Desk: Workplace Issues for LGBTQ Librarians* (Sacramento, CA: Library Juice Press, 2011).

14. Donna Braquet and Roger Weaver, "Out All Over: Giving Voice to LGBTs on Campus," in *Out Behind the Desk: Workplace Issues for LGBTQ Librarians*, ed. Tracy Nectoux, (Sacramento, CA: Library Juice Press, 2011), 79.

15. Marcia M. Gallo, "To Barbara Gittings, 1932-2007: Thank You."*Gay & Lesbian Review Worldwide* (May 2007), 7-8.

to physical movement, patterns of cognition, or who one is attracted to. When a mobility-impaired person criticizes the way that they move, it is coming from an internalized standard that is somewhat arbitrary. That suggests that holding somebody's private decisions up for criticism is also using an arbitrary standard.

The story of Sharon Kowalski represents the true value of legal recognition for same-sex couples: to protect the rights of someone who becomes disabled. Same-sex couples must be allowed to choose caregivers and who has legal guardianship, in case of disabling accident or illness. This is a basic human right.

Is it possible to spot someone who is disabled? Our own particular version of "gaydar" ("cripdar?") is very similar. If you consider the authors' discussion of invisible disabilities, it is very clear that some disabilities can be easily spotted, but many cannot. The authors have learned to make no assumptions, whether it is in the workplace, or an elevator, or a parking lot. It is impossible to tell if somebody is disabled. The prevalence of invisible disabilities is one of the major takeaways of this study.

7. FEMINISM AND DISABILITY

The relationship between feminism and disability begins with the understanding that femaleness has been described in terms that equate it with disability.[1] There is also a literature by disabled feminists, calling out disabled studies for focusing on men, and calling out the feminist movement for having no room for the disabled.[2] Begum takes a look at "gender roles, self-image and sexuality."[3] In each case she points out how these traditional feminist issues have particular resonance for disabled women.

Thomas points out "feminist fragmentation," referring to the differences of experience, depending on class, race, and / or sexual preference.[4] This connects with this book's concern relating to the complexity of identity and it illustrates a gap in the feminist literature. Audre Lorde, a remarkable black

---

1. Rosemarie Garland Thomson, "Integrating Disability, Transforming Feminist Theory," in *Feminist Disability Studies,* ed. Kim Q. Hall (Bloomington, IN: Indiana University Press, 2011), 18; Natalie A. Dykstra, "'Trying to Idle': Work and Disability in the Diary of Alice James" in *The New Disability History: American Perspectives,* edited by Paul K. Longmore, and Lauri Umansky, (New York: NYU Press, 2001), 108; Jenny Morris *Pride Against Prejudice: A Personal Politics Of Disability* (London: Women's Press, 1991), 98.

2. Nasa Begum, "Disabled Women and the Feminist Aggenda," *Feminist Review* 40, no. 1 (1992): 70-84.

3. Begum, "Disabled Women." 70.

4. Carol Thomas, *Female Forms: Experiencing and Understanding Disability.* (Buckingham, UK: Open University Press, 1999): 102.

feminist writer, makes a strong case for the complexity of identity, but does not mention disability.[5] Likewise, Susan Bordo does not mention disability.[6]

This is confirmed by Jenny Morris, who writes extensively about the "relevance" of feminism to "disabled politics."[7] "Disability and old age are aspects of identity with which gender is very much entwined and they are identities which have been entirely ignored by feminists."[8]

Bonnie Sher Klein has a unique voice as a veteran feminist, who then survived a stoke: "I feel as if my colleagues are ashamed of me because I am no longer the image of strength, competence, and independence that feminists, including myself, are so eager to project. There is clearly a conflict between feminism's rhetoric of inclusion and failure to include disability."[9] This is parallel to the realization that mainstream second-wave feminism was also recognized as being very white and middle class.[10]

Feminists discuss many issues that are of critical importance to disabled women. An excellent example is

---

5. Audre Lorde, "Age, Race, Class, and Sex: Women Redefining Difference," in *Sister Outsider: Essays and Speeches,* (Berkeley. CA: Crossing Press, 2007): 113-123.

6. Susan Bordo, *Unbearable Weight: Feminism, Western Culture, and the Body* (Berkeley, CA: University of California Press, 2004).

7. Morris, *Pride Against Prejudice,* 9.

8. Morris, *Pride Against Prejudice,* 7.

9. Bonnie Sherr Klein, "'We Are Who You Are': Feminism and Disability," *Ms.* 3, no.3 (1992): 72.

10. Patricia Hill Collins, *Black Feminist Thought: Knowledge, Consciousness, and the Politics of Empowerment.* (New York: Routledge, 2000), 5-6.

Naomi Wolf.[11] Wolf describes the idea of a "professional beauty qualification."[12] This is alarming to those with visible disabilities. The literature that addresses questions of body image is very thought-provoking for any woman with visible disabilities.[13]

Susan Wendell writes about the "idealization of the body" in consumerist society.[14] This is closely connected to what she describes as "the disciplines of femininity."[15] When physical ideals are impossible to reach, this makes the disabled outsiders.[16]

Judith Butler writes about how gender is defined, "What is gender, how is it produced and reproduced?"[17] The implication of performativity is that gender is external, it is a performance. Can we get past being judged by our ability to perform our designated/accepted gender role along accepted lines? This comes back to the issues raised by Wolf and others. Some of the trappings of femininity are not available to all disabled women (high heels, make up, etc.).

Butler's work draws out common threads between feminism, queer studies, and disability studies. "This is the

---

11. Naomi Wolf, *The Beauty Myth: How Images of Beauty Are Used Against Women.* (New York: Perennial, 2002).

12. Wolf, *The Beauty Myth* 27.

13. Bordo, *Unbearable Weight;* Megan Jayne Crabbe, *Body Positive Power* (London: Vermillion, 2018).

14. Wendell, *Rejected Body,* 88.

15. Wendell, 88.

16. Wendell, 91.

17. Judith Butler, *Gender Trouble: Feminism and the Subversion of Identity* (New York: Routledge, 1999), 23.

positive, normative task in Gender Trouble, it is to insist upon the extension of this legitimacy to bodies that have been regarded as false, unreal and unintelligible."[18] A few disabilities studies scholars have worked with Butler's ideas.[19] Kim Davies owns that Butler has paid "little explicit attention . . . to disability," but nevertheless uses performativity as a frame for discussing Asperger's Syndrome.[20]

Caregiving

The needs of the disabled also intersect with feminism when considering the literature of caregiving. Caregiving has multiple facets. Feminist theorists have confronted the persistent demand that women are expected to be the caregivers.[21] Often the disabled are not taken seriously as potential mothers, able to give care to a young child.[22] Some people with disabilities are in need of personal care attendants themselves.[23]

18. Butler, *Gender Trouble*, 23.

19. Kim Davies, "A Troubled Identity: Putting Butler to Work on the Comings and Goings of Asperger's Syndrome," in *Disability Studies: Educating for Inclusion,* ed. Tim Corcoran, Julie White, and Ben Whitburn (Boston: Sense Publishers, 2015) 197.

20. Davies, "A Troubled Identity," 198.

21. Janet Finch, "Community Care: Developing Non-Sexist Alternatives," *Critical Social Policy* 3, no. 9 (1983): 6-18.

22, Denise Sherer Jacobson, *The Question of David; A Disabled Mother's Journey Through Adoption, Family and Life. (*Berkeley, CA: Creative Arts Book Co, 1999.); Begum, "Agenda," 74.

23, Connie Panzarino, *The Me in the Mirror.* (Seattle, WA: Seal Press, 1994).

Discussion

The journey into feminist literature was a powerful experience. Many of these sources have deeply affected the authors, and the frustration of the disabled community with feminism has been very clear. In particular the performative nature of gender is something that has always haunted Brown, because some of the aspects of femininity are just not available to her. "Girl shoes," for example, are not usable.

The issue of caregiving was not addressed by this study. Our respondents were able to work. The question of how much help is needed at home and who provides it was not addressed. Some of the interviews did lead to some personal conversations about being a disabled parent.

Race and Feminism

The literature of feminism has been deeply impacted by white privilege. The initial idea of femaleness being a disability appears ridiculous, when contrasted with the experiences of women of color.[1] What are the appropriate issues to be tackled by feminists? Mikki Kendall encourages her readers to think about gun control, hunger, poverty, housing, and educational discrimination, all as feminist issues.[2] Through this lens, feminism is converted into human rights.

---

1. Mikki Kendall, *Hood Feminism: Notes from the Women That a Movement Forgot* (New York: Viking, 2020), 8.

2. Kendall, *Hood Feminism.*

8. Race, Disability Studies, and Intersectionality

Our interest in looking at disabilities and multiple identities really began while reading Erevelles and Minear.[1] They make a strong case for the intersection of race and disability. They describe the challenge faced by "[f]eminists of color… attempting to theorize oppression faced at the multiple fronts of race, class, gender, sexuality, and disability."[2] Erevelles and Minear are responding to Williams.[3] Williams describes "racism as a crime, an offense so deeply painful and assaultive as to constitute something I call 'spirit-murder.'"[4] Pursuing the ideas they presented led the authors to a rich literature on intersectionality and critical race theory.

Intersectionality is a term that was originally offered by Crenshaw, when looking at the intersection of sexism and racism.[5] One of the most important writers on intersectionality

---

1. Nirmala Erevelles and Andrea Minear, "Unspeakable Offenses: Untangling Race and Disability in Discourses of Intersectionality," *Journal of Literary & Cultural Disability Studies* 4, no. 2 (2010): 127-145.

2. Erevelles and Minear, "Unspeakable Offenses," 129.

3. Patricia Williams, "Spirit-Murdering the Messenger: The Discourse of Finger Pointing as the Law's Response to Racism," *University of Miami Law Review* 42 (1987): 127-157.

4. Williams, "Spirit-Murdering the Messenger,"129.

5. Kimberlé Crenshaw, "Mapping the Margins: Intersectionality, Identity Politics, and Violence Against Women of Color," *Stanford Law Review* 43 (1990): 1241-1299.

is Patricia Hill Collins.[6] She places disability alongside other complex themes that make up identity. Collins and Bilge observed that "…race, class, gender, sexuality, age, disability, ethnicity, nation, and religion, among others, constitute interlocking, mutually constructing or intersecting systems of power."[7] Pastrana makes an interesting observation, based on his study of LGBT leaders of color: "Within systems of oppression people are surviving and thriving."[8]

It has been acknowledged that racism and ableism often are "both multiple and simultaneous" systems of power.[9] The commonalities between experiences of racism and experiences of ableism are the focus of Asch's work.[10] In particular, considering the basic principle that racism is embedded in our culture, which creates a new understanding of how difficult it is to dislodge ableism.

When looking at the broader question of race and disability, it is important to acknowledge the research that was done by Artiles, who looked at the use of intellectual and cognitive diagnoses as being disproportionately applied to young people

---

6. Patricia Hill Collins and Sirma Bilge, *Intersectionality* (Malden, MA: Polity Press, 2016).

7. Collins and Bilge, *Intersectionality*, 27.

8. Antonio Pastrana Jr., "Privileging Oppression: Contradictions in Intersectional Politics," *Western Journal of Black Studies* 34, no. 1 (2010): 63.

9. Ayesha Vernon, "Fighting Two Different Battles: Unity is Preferable to Enmity," in *Disability Studies: Past, Present and Future,* edited by Len Barton & Mike Oliver (Leeds, UK: Disability Press, 1997), 257.

10. Adrienne Asch, "Critical Race Theory, Feminism, and Disability: Reflections on Social Justice and Personal Identity," *Ohio State Law Journal* 62 (2001): 391-423.

of color.[11] Annamma et al. provides an excellent introduction to the intersection of race and disability in education, and the research that has begun to call out this issue.[12]

Race and Library Workers

Morales, Knowles, and Bourg tackle the major issue of the lack of diversity within the library profession, despite the fact that national demographics are changing.[13] Social justice activists in libraries have also tackled problematic knowledge structures.[14] Walker offers an overview of the problems encountered by librarians of color in the pursuit of an academic career. [15] She offers critical race theory (CRT), as a framework for the challenges faced by academic librarians of color. In a way that is similar to the early feminist statement

11. Alfredo J. Artiles, "Untangling the Racialization of Disabilities: An Intersectionality Critique Across Disability Models," *Du Bois Review: Social Science Research on Race* 10, no. 2 (2013): 329-347.

12. Subini Ancy Annamma, David J. Connor, and Beth Ferri, "Dis/ability Critical Race Studies (DisCrit): Theorizing at the Intersections of Race and Dis/ability," in *DisCrit: Disability Studies and Critical Race Theory in Education,* eds. David J. Connor, Beth A. Ferri and Subini A. Annamma (New York: Teacher's College Press, 2016), 9-32.

13. Myrna, Morales, Em Claire Knowles, and Chris Bourg, "Diversity, Social Justice, and the Future of Libraries, *Portal: Libraries and the Academy* 14, no. 3 (2014): 441.

14. Morales, Knowles and Bourg, "Diversity," 445.

15. Shaundra Walker, "Critical Race Theory and the Recruitment, Retention and Promotion of a Librarian of Color: A Counterstory," in *Where Are All Librarians of Color? The Experiences of People of Color in Academia,* ed. Rebecca Hankins & Miguel Juárez (Sacramento, CA: Library Juice Press, 2015), 135-160.

that "the personal is political,"[16] Walker emphasizes that CRT acknowledges "experiential knowledge."[17]

Hankins reminds her readers that the issue of racial disparities within libraries is "symptomatic of society as a whole."[18] Brook et al. also review the impact of "white institutional presence" on academic libraries, stressing actions that all librarians can take to move toward social justice.[19] Brook's work is important, although the authors found that it does not acknowledge Historically Black Colleges and Universities and other colleges that were founded to serve minority students.

Moore and Estrellado mention an issue that should be taken into account when examining the intersection between race and libraries. Among people of color who become librarians, many "spend significant years working as staff."[20]

Dewey introduces the significant work that the Association of Research Libraries (ARL) has done to increase

---

16. Carol Hanisch, "The Personal is Political," (1969), http://www.carolhanisch.org/CHwritings/PersonalIsPol.pdf

17. Walker, "Critical Race Theory," 155.

18. Rebecca Hankins, "Racial Realism or Foolish Optimism: An African American Muslim Woman in the Field," in *Where are All Librarians of Color? The Experiences of People of Color in Academia,* ed. Rebecca Hankins & Miguel Juárez, (Sacramento, CA: Library Juice Press, 2015), 209.

19. Freeda Brook, Dave Ellenwood, and Althea Eannace Lazzaro, "In Pursuit of Antiracist Social Justice: Denaturalizing Whiteness in the Academic Library," *Library Trends* 64, no. 2 (2015): 251.

20. Alanna Moore and Jan Estrellado, "Identity, Activism, Self-Care, and Women of Color Librarians," in *Pushing the Margin: Women of Color and Intersectionality in LIS,* ed. Rose L. Chou, and Annie Pho (Sacramento, CA: Litwin Books, 2018), 363.

diversity among library faculty and staff.[21] It is important to acknowledge that introducing an early career librarian of color to what may be a non-diverse university is fraught with challenges.[22] Anantachai et al. make a very strong recommendation for a diverse community, and a systematic effort to find support networks, both within the university and through national and international service.[23]

Racism and Health Care

Schomberg reminds her readers that: "Poverty, racism, sexism and other social ills increase the types of trauma that can cause mental health problems and chronic illnesses."[24]

There is a connection between race and disablement. Kafer states that health care disparities lead to a higher level of disablement among African Americans.[25] Sack reported on research that shows the impacts of both race and location on

---

21. Barbara I. Dewey, "The Imperative for Diversity: ARL's Progress and Role," *Portal: Libraries and the Academy* 9, no. 3 (2009): 355-361.

22. Jason K. Alson, "Interns or Professionals? A Common Misnomer Applied to Diversity Resident Librarians Can Potentially Degrade and Divide," in *Where Are All the Librarians of Color? The Experiences of People of Color in Academia* ed. Rebecca Hankins and Miguel Juárez (Sacramento, CA: Library Juice Press, 2015), 71-93.

23. Tarida Anantachai, et al., "Establishing a Communal Network for Professional Advancement among Librarians of Color," in *Where Are All the Librarians of Color? The Experiences of People of Color in Academia,* ed. Rebecca Hankins and Miguel Juárez (Sacramento, CA: Library Juice Press, 2015), 31-53.

24. Schomberg, "Disability at Work," 115

25. Allison Kafer, *Feminist, Queer, Crip* (Bloomington, IN: Indiana University Press, 2013), 33-34.

health outcomes.[26] Roberts writes extensively on the social and political nature of race, and the health consequences of racism.[27]

Privilege

Peggy McIntosh is an academic and an anti-racism activist. She is a leader in the field of privilege studies.[28] It is important to acknowledge the profound work of Peggy McIntosh on white privilege.[29] As a white, heterosexual, cisgender female, Brown found her description of the contents of the "invisible knapsack" (a metaphor that describes the privileges that white, middle-class members of society receive automatically) to be very thought provoking.[30] Lewis Gordon offers a very thought provoking critique of the idea of white privilege. The privileges that are accorded to white people, are not privileges, they are human rights.[31] The field of privilege studies confirms the very important work of anti-racism.

26. Kevin Sack, "Research Finds Wide Disparities in Health Care by Race and Region," *New York Times* 5 June 2008: A18(L).

27. Dorothy Roberts, *Fatal Invention: How Science, Politics, and Big Business Re-Create Race in the Twenty-First Century* (New York: The New Press, 2011).

28. Peggy McIntosh, "Reflections and Future Directions for Privilege Studies," *Journal of Social Issues* 68, no. 1 (2012): 194-206.

29. Peggy McIntosh, *On Privilege, Fraudulence, and Teaching as Learning: Selected Essays 1981-2019,* (New York: Routledge, 2020).

30. McIntosh, *On Privilege,* 29-34.

31. Lewis R. Gordon, "White Privilege and the Problem with Affirmative Action," in *"I Don't See Color": Personal and Critical Perspectives on White Privilege.* eds. Bettina Bergo and Tracey Nicholls (University Park, PA: Pennsylvania State University Press, 2015), 27.

This is not an easy journey. Robin DiAngelo carefully describes why anti-racism training is so difficult for white people.[32]

History

The history of segregated public library service in the Jim Crow South is being explored by historians.[33] Knott makes it very clear that segregated public libraries were part of the systematic segregation of Southern society. The African American community cared very deeply about the value of education and founded libraries for their communities across the South, often facing fierce opposition.

Discussion

The authors have observed the racial disparity between librarians and staff that plagues many libraries. If one wishes to capture a true picture of the impact of disabilities in the library work force, all should be included. The phrase "library workers" is meant to be inclusive in the current work. When the authors had decided to do a survey of disabled library workers for this book, they wanted to address issues of disability, demographics, race, and sexual preferences. They

---

32. Robin DiAngelo, "White Fragility," *International Journal of Critical Pedagogy* 3, no. 3 (2011): 54-70.

33. Cheryl Knott, *Not Free, Not for All: Public Libraries in the Age of Jim Crow* (Boston: University of Massachusetts Press, 2016); Toby Graham Patterson, *A Right to Read: Segregation and Civil Rights in Alabama's Public Libraries, 1900-1965* (Tuscaloosa, AL: University of Alabama Press, 2002); Shirley A. Wiegand and Wayne A. Wiegand, *The Desegregation of Public Libraries in the Jim Crow South: Civil Rights and Local Activism* (Baton Rouge, LA: LSU Press, 2018).

expect that this will create a more comprehensive picture of the disabled library community than currently exists.

The history of public library service in the United States, where it intersected with segregation, is difficult. For readers who would like to get a journal article-length overview of the desegregation process, we recommend Cresswell.[34] We mention it here because it must be acknowledged, along with the fact that issues of institutional racism are still deeply concerning.

There are often moments in reading writers of color when a connection between racism and ableism jumps out, with the call to stand together. Alice Walker, who grew up with a visual impairment, spoke of loneliness.[35] Loneliness is one of the undergirding issues of this research. A concern about ableism has led us to a deeper commitment to anti-racism. This makes it easier to stand with others who are in the struggle against racism. Artiles and other researchers and writers describe an educational system that uses ableism to discriminate against children of color. This is fundamentally a social justice issue.

We believe the disabled community can also learn from the work of Anantachai et al.[36] Disabled library workers need to work on building supportive networks (see chapter 11 on Advocacy). There are deep connections between anti-racism and disabilities activism. It is acknowledged in the literature

---

34. Stephen Cresswell, "The Last Days of Jim Crow in Southern Libraries," *Libraries & culture* (1996): 557-573.

35. Alice Walker, "From an Interview," in *In Search of Our Mother's Gardens* (New York: Harcourt Brace), 244.

36. Anantachai et al., "Establishing."

that disabilities studies is a "white" subject.[37] OToole makes a very strong case for the work that needs to be done to diversify disabilities studies. There is a dramatic need for disabilities activism to be reinvigorated, to address "structural inequalities."[38] Gibson et al. remind us that neutrality is not possible.[39] To know what it means to be "other," pulls us into identifying with others. What is anti-racism? Kendi states that anti-racism is a positive act, a deep commitment to actively "recognize the reality of biological equality, that skin color is…meaningless."[40] Anti-racism actively opposes racism, and seeks fundamental equality.

37. Chris Bell, "Is Disability Studies Actually White Disability Studies?" *Disability Studies Reader* (5th ed.), edited by Lennard Davis (New York: Routledge: 2017), 404-415.

38. OToole, *Fading Scars*, 93.

39. Gibson et al., "Libraries on the Frontlines: Neutrality and Social Justice," *Equality, Diversity and Inclusion: An International Journal* 36, no. 8 (2017): 751-766.

40. Ibram X. Kendi, *How to Be an Antiracist* (New York: One World, 2019), 54.

9. How Does This Impact Our Patrons? Inclusive Libraries

Our research is on disabled library workers. In the process of the literature review, we found that many of the same issues and principles also affect disabled library patrons. When Pionke interviewed patrons on the autism spectrum, problems were reported that are similar to the communication problems reported in our interviews.[1] Flink describes the challenges faced by student veterans with invisible disabilities.[2] The problems faced by student veterans with invisible disabilities are similar to the problems faced by library workers with invisible disabilities seeking employment.

Sheidlower describes the long history of library service to the disabled.[3] This stresses that service to all library patrons has been a part of library service from the beginning.

---

1. J.J. Pionke. "Toward Holistic Accessibility: Narratives from Functionally Diverse Patrons," *Reference & User Services Quarterly* 57, no. 1 (Fall 2017): 48-56.

2. Patrick J. Flink, "Invisible Disabilities, Stigma, and Student Veterans: Contextualizing the Transition to Higher Education," *Journal of Veterans Studies* 2, no. 2 (2017): 110-120.

3. Scott Sheidlower, "Accommodating the Disabled in Library One-Shots at York College/CUNY," *Codex, the Journal of the Louisiana Chapter of the ACRL*, 4, no. 3 (2017), 65.

One of the major concerns for academic libraries is the legal requirement to make the library's public web presence fully accessible. Leonard describes the work that her library did to work through a complaint from the federal Office of Civil Rights in relationship to their public web presence.[4] Remy and Seaman make a very important point that clarifies how to approach inclusive library services: "The potential lack of disclosure [by patrons with invisible disabilities] underscores the need for libraries to holistically examine services and programs."[5] Universal Design covers many aspects of libraries. Universal Design is a useful framework for examining services and programs to make sure that all patrons are served. The National Education Association stresses the following principles of Universal Design (UD): "equitable use, flexibility in use, simple and intuitive, perceptible information, tolerance for error, low physical effort, size and space for approach, a community of learners, and instructional climate."[6] For example, many people find elevators and ramps useful; stairs are an impediment to some. A reference desk influenced by UD would have variable heights, to meet the needs of everybody without having to come around the desk.

---

4. Elizabeth Leonard, "Dream the Impossible Dream: A Case Study of US Federal Website Accessibility Standards Compliance at Seton Hall University Libraries," *International Information and Library Review* 50, no. 1 (2018): 34-39.

5. Charlie Remy and Priscilla Seaman, "Evolving from Disability to Diversity: How to Better Serve High-Functioning Autistic Students," *Reference & User Services Quarterly* 54, no. 1 (2014): 25.

6. "Understanding Universal Design in the Classroom", National Education Association, accessed January 23, 2020, http://www.nea.org/home/34693.htm.

One of the most important opportunities for implementing structural Universal Design is when a library is in the midst of a renovation project. It's important to involve library patrons with disabilities in the design process.[7]

Universal Design is also important when considering the educational role of libraries and librarians. Universal Design for Learning (UDL) is an educational movement that is focused on changing our instructional practices to reach the maximum number of students. The concept is to understand how instruction goes together and make it as flexible as possible. There are three strands or facets involved: multiple means of engagement, multiple means of representation, and multiple means of action and expression.[8]

Webb and Hoover offer a case study, describing how they applied multiple means of representation to a web-based biology tutorial project.[9] Zhong wrote about a useful structure for a face-to-face lesson plan that follows UDL guidelines.[10]

Discussion

Many of the principles discussed in this book apply equally well to disabled library patrons. There is a need for empathy

---

7. Carli Spina, "Libraries and Universal Design," *Theological Librarianship* 10, no. 1 (October 2017), 6.

8. "Universal Design for Learning Guidelines" CAST (2018), Version 2.2, accessed January 23, 2020, http://udlguidelines.cast.org.

9. Katy Kavanagh Webb and Jeanne Hoover, "Universal Design for Learning (UDL) in the Academic Library: A Methodology for Mapping Multiple Means of Representation in Library Tutorials," *College & Research Libraries* 76, no. 4 (2015): 537-553.

10. Ying Zhong, "Universal Design for Learning (UDL) in Library Instruction," *College & Undergraduate Libraries* 19, no. 1 (2012): 36-40.

and flexibility, because you don't always know what is going on with the person you are interacting with. Using Universal Design principles to design services and structures means that people don't have to necessarily self-identify to get their needs met. Requiring people to self-identify, and solving problems on a case-by-case basis, is a source of stress for all involved. We would like to encourage our readers to use the principles of Universal Design to create holistic, caring library services.

10. Findings

The survey was begun in March, 2019. This study, as it has evolved, searched for and found disabled library workers working in all different types of libraries. Professor Brown wrote to the president of each state library association. Often the survey invitation was placed on the local listserv. This was done to try and reach public librarians. It was often successful, noticeable because of a cluster of answers received in a short period of time from a particular state. As of July, 2019, 227 people had answered the survey. All that was required to participate was to self-identify as a person with a disability. Interviews were conducted widely with many of the people who expressed a willingness to be interviewed (46 people were interviewed, and an additional 6 people submitted written responses to the interview questions).

None of the questions were required, so the percentages that follow are marked with the number of people who answered the question and do not always add up to 100%. What follows is a quantitative demographics section, followed by major themes that came up in the data analysis. Excerpts from the interviews are included, identified by single quotes.

How do we self-identify?
- The first question in the survey used general categories to find out more about the types of disabilities being reported. Most notable was the level of mental health issues reported by our respondents. Psychological issues were reported by 30% (38) of 127 respondents

who answered that question. We also noted that problems with "energy levels" were reported by 22% of 127 (29). Mobility issues were identified by 37.7% of 127 respondents (48). Many respondents identified multiple issues. It was not unusual for people to identify both visible and invisible disabilities.

We asked the people we interviewed to identify why they self-identified as being disabled. The answers were striking in their variety. Five described cerebral palsy, which covers a wide range of impacts. Two identified as amputees, due to bone cancer. Four have hearing loss, and four have low vision. There were several conversations about chronic illness, and nine people mentioned mental health issues. Three people out of 52 spoke of using a wheelchair. Keeping in mind that 223 is not a definitive survey, it demonstrates the variety of people who self-identify as disabled. Although the international symbol of disability is a person in a wheelchair, most people who need accommodations are not people who use wheelchairs.

Layers of identity
- race / ethnicity (188 respondents)

The issue of race and libraries has been previously discussed (see chapter 8). The profile of our respondents is similar to the statistics gathered by ALA. (For example, according to Diversity Counts 2012 Tables, just over 5% of credentialed librarians are African American.)

♦80.85% of our respondents identified as White/ Caucasian (157)
♦African American 4.79% (9)

- ♦ Multiracial 2.3% (5)
- ♦ Hispanic / Latino 3.72% (6)
- ♦ Native American 2.13% (5)
- ♦ Asian Pacific Islander 1.6% (3)

- Gender (220 respondents)
  - ♦79.5% Female (175)
  - ♦10.9% Male (24)
  - ♦2.7% Prefer not to say (6)
  - ♦3.64% Non-binary (8)
  - ♦2.27% Genderqueer(5)
  - ♦.45% Transgender (1)

We are glad people who are not cis-gendered felt comfortable enough to step forward. In spite of it being 2020 such people are not always accepted by friends and families. In the interviews, some expressed that the need to support themselves was even more important because of family estrangement.
- Do you identify as LGBTQIA? (224)
  - ♦57.6 % No (129)
  - ♦38.8% Yes (87)

If yes, has this identity intersected with your work in libraries?
The most common intersection that came up in interviews was the opportunity to help build the library collections in this area.
- If yes, are you out in the library? (105)
  - ♦38.1% No (40)
  - ♦42.9% Yes (45)
  - ♦19% Maybe (20)

- What is your job in your library?

There was no typical response. Interviews were conducted with library directors, department heads, early career librarians, and library staff.

- What year did you graduate from library school? (174)

We recognize that we also talked to library staff. That's why the number of people responding to this question is lower. Many of our respondents are new librarians (graduating within the last ten years). This underlines the importance of the Americans with Disabilities Act in expanding access of disabled people to professional careers. Two of the people interviewed were entering or applying to online library degree programs, an important innovation for people with a variety of disabilities because it lets them learn and more easily accommodates their disability.

> ◆5.17% (8) of the respondents are current library school students.
>
> ◆43% (77) of the respondents are new librarians.

Themes from the Interviews

The authors themselves have generally visible primary disabilities. One of the first true surprises was the number of respondents who identified as having invisible disabilities. A significant number of respondents reported invisible disabilities including depleted energy level, sensory disability, and psychological disability. Fatigue was a topic that often came up during the interviews. About 30% of our respondents identified mental health as a major impairment. This has profound implications for compassion in the workplace. Invisible disabilities are very common and difficult to spot. This ties in with the challenge of managing expectations. We found that expectations are a true challenge for people with invisible disabilities.

→'Difficult to describe my needs. People are not aware that I feel sick. It can be difficult to advocate. I am telling the truth.'

→'Physical illness is easier to explain than psychiatric problems.'

→'It's harder to have an invisible disability.'

This came up in multiple interviews. Managing the expectations of supervisors, particularly if the choice has been made to not self-identify, was identified as difficult. Expectations are also connected with empathy. The true need is for creating a culture of empathy within libraries among colleagues and with the public. This also touches on relationships with supervisors.

Communication is Harder Than It Looks
Most of the challenges identified in interviews came down to communication issues. For example, communication is a challenge when you are legally blind because, among other things, you cannot see non-verbal cues. There are a whole range of issues that can create auditory perception problems. Learning disabilities and life on the autism spectrum are mainly about communication problems.

'The Dialogue'
Quotidian communication with co-workers and supervisors about impairments can be difficult. One respondent left a position rather than self-identify, because they could no longer do what they were being asked to do. This risk was very

real, since they worked in a library that was too small to be covered by the Americans with Disabilities Act. Progressive hearing loss was also described as 'maddening,' making both public service and interaction with co-workers extraordinarily difficult.

→'some patrons don't take me seriously'

Problems with patrons also showed up in the interviews. A library staff person in a wheelchair may not be taken seriously. Public service is difficult with hearing loss. In that case the public are 'intrusive and not empathetic.'

→'It takes a lot of energy to behave in a way that is expected.'

The Sweet Spot

There are multiple possible sources of stress in the complex world of providing library services as a person with a disability. However, with the right combination of factors, library workers with disabilities can discover extraordinary career stability. Given the right combination of empathetic managers and accessible infrastructure, it's difficult to imagine looking for another job. It's not worth the risk. Among our respondents there were people who had been in their library system for many years, benefiting from internal hires. The authors can identify with this phenomenon.

→[Current place is] 'willing to work with me where I am at'
→'Somewhat stuck'
♦20.5% 5-10 years (46 of 224)
♦24.1% over 10 years (54 of 220)

Career Expectations
This is connected to stability. Often it is easier to stay put, with a manageable level of stress, than to try and move up within the library system. Some library workers are unable to change positions because the next level of responsibility requires travel around their system, and they have no public transportation in that area and they do not drive.

Stability does not always happen. Several of the people that were interviewed were in transition, having changed to a different kind of library, or a different type of job.

In an Ideal World
One of the interview questions asked was: What would you do differently, vis-à-vis your manager? Not all situations were ideal. Challenging situations could be mitigated by improved empathy and improved communication with management. This came up multiple times during the interviews.

→'I would like to live in a world where you could tell your manager [about one's disability].'

→'There is no handbook…outlining the library's policies toward employees with disabilities.'

Some spoke of a desire for more flexibility. This is connected to empathy and compassion.

→'In an ideal world: I could be a lot more productive if I could do 'Telework' — if I could be left out of the social drama.'

→'[I would like] more protections in place. More flexibility.'

→'Ideally [my manager] could talk to me about shortcomings. Dialogue about what could be done differently.'

→'ask for my input about accessibility issues before they happen.'

Some of the comments in the interviews were very moving:

→'People who have disabilities are just as valuable as the other employees. Treating people as equals.'

→'understand that while I identify as having these conditions, they don't define me.'

→'Worry about accommodations means pity.'

To balance the challenges, it's important to point out that many disabled library workers are remarkably stable and show up each day as valued members of their library community.

→'My director is great because she's very flexible and respects people's individuality and autonomy.'

11. ADVOCACY

Emancipatory Research

Emancipatory research is a movement connected to the social model of disability. Stone and Priestly postulate that the social model of disability rejects the location of disability within the body in the way that feminism identifies oppression within patriarchy. [1] Within this lens, disability is a form of oppression—hence the deep concern about the purpose of disability studies research. "This means a commitment to a social science that can change the world as well as describe it."[2]

Some of the literature on disabilities studies and emancipatory research does not accept the possibility that the researchers are themselves disabled.[3] Advocates of emancipatory research believe that the research should be of "practical benefit" to the community of which the research is

---

1. Emma Stone and Mark Priestley, "Parasites, Pawns and Partners: Disability Research And The Role Of Non-Disabled Researchers," *British Journal of Sociology* 47, no. 4 (1996): 699.

2. Joan Acker, Kate Barry, and Joke Esseveld, "Objectivity and Truth: Problems in Doing Feminist Research" in *Beyond Methodology: Feminist Scholarship as Lived Research,* ed. Mary Margaret Fonow, and Judith A. Cook (Bloomington, IN: Indiana University Press, 1991), 134.

3. Gerry Zarb, "On the Road to Damascus: First Steps towards Changing the Relations of Disability Research Production," *Disability, Handicap & Society* 7, no. 2 (1992): 125–38.

about.[4] Using this call, how can one change the world? First, the authors acknowledge that this type of research has been of tremendous benefit to themselves, as self-identified disabled library workers. The authors have found a community and grown in self-understanding. The discovery of the literature on emancipatory research really woke the authors up to some of the problems and potentials of doing social science research in this field. How can the authors and the readers avoid seeing this volume as a volume of "mere self-description"?[5]

"Will it achieve any[thing] more than furthering academic careers and publication lists?"[6] Wescott makes the same point in a feminist critique of social science: we must have "an intention for the future rather than a resignation to the present. The intention is not a historical inevitability but a vision."[7]

This can be deeply inspiring and might become the work of a lifetime. With that as the frame, what follows are some of the themes that appeared in our survey and interviews.

Equity, Diversity, and Inclusion
Annamma et al. describe the complex relationship between racism and ableism.[8] Ruiz reminds us that, if we are going to fight ableism, we must not neglect "fighting racism, fighting

---

4. Stone and Priestley, "Parasites," 706.

5. Stone and Priestley, "Parasites," 705.

6. Stone and Priestley, "Parasites," 702.

7. Marcia Westkott, "Feminist Criticism of the Social Sciences," *Harvard Educational Review* 49, no. 4 (1979): 428.

8. Annamma et al., "Dis/Crit," 14.

classism, fighting homophobia; you can't take them apart."[9] The authors began to present on not trusting first impressions, because invisible disabilities are impossible to spot. This touches on not judging anybody by surface appearances. This is equity, diversity, and inclusion on all levels. Everyone should consider what it means to not judge anybody by surface appearances.

Infrastructure

There are many passionate, creative people who do not drive. Some cannot due to sensory impairments. That means that they are significantly limited in terms of where they can work. Mass transit is a very basic accessibility issue. It is important to provide mass transit in a way that it can be used by everybody. As mentioned by Hunter-Zaworski, the aging population is also in need of innovative transportation solutions.[10] In this era when everybody is talking about the small actions we can take to help the environment, the authors call on communities to consider providing mass transit. This can be as simple as "community buses."[11] It will tremendously expand the labor pool. Libraries will also become more available to members of the public if they can get there without driving. Society needs to stop privileging the driver.

While considering infrastructure, it is necessary to take a look at a very useful tool, the elevator. O'Brien reminds

---

9. Ruiz, "Violence," 239.

10. Katharine Hunter-Zaworski, "Getting Around in an Aging Society," *Planning* 73, no. 5 (2007): 22-25.

11. Hunter-Zaworski, "Getting Around," 24.

us that elevators are useful for a great many people.[12] This ties in closely with the current popular movement, "Elevators are for everyone."[13] They are focused on the fact that many of the citizens of New York City are shuffled off to Access-a-Ride, which is a separate but not equal van-based mass transit system.[14]

New York City is in the midst of a contentious conversation about the accessibility of the subway system. New York City has one of the largest subway systems in the world, and only a fraction of the stations are accessible. Several disability advocacy organizations have sued the Metropolitan Transportation Authority (MTA) which runs the system.[15] The risks presented by this situation were underlined in January, 2019, when a young mother died after falling while trying to carry her daughter's stroller down the subway stairs.[16]

Brown rides a lot of elevators. She is there with her rollator, along with bicycles, strollers, delivery services, and luggage

12. Ruth O'Brien, *Crippled Justice: The History of Modern Disability Policy in the Workplace* (Chicago: University of Chicago Press, 2001), 2.

13. "Rise and Resist: Elevator Action Group," Rise and Resist, accessed January 31, 2020, https://www.riseandresist.org/elevator-action-group.

14. "NYLPI and Disability Rights Partners Launch New Coalition," NYLPI, accessed January 31, 2020, https://nylpi.org/nylpi-and-disability-rights-partners-launch-new-coalition-aarrg-the-access-a-ride-reform-group-calling-on-the-mta-to-fix-horrendous-conditions-and-reform-service-which-contributes-to-high-unemplo/

15. Eli Rosenberg, "New York City's Subway System Violates Local and Federal Laws, Disability Groups Say," *New York Times,* April 25, 2017.

16. Michael Gold and Emma G. Fitzsimmons, "Young Mother, Hauling Child and Stroller Down Subway Steps, Dies," *New York Times,* January 30, 2019.

of various types. In addition, there are always people who do not have signs on them, explaining why they need to use the elevator. Elevators are an important tool for everybody. The authors have not found any research that backs up this assertion. There is some traction for the opposite assertion: elevators are bad for your health. That idea is to motivate college students to use stairs more often than the elevator.[17] This works for some people but leaves out a section of the population.

Elevators are for everybody. If we listen to people who are using elevators, it seems perfectly obvious. The authors want to think about how to document this.

Politics

The World Health Organization (WHO) has created a benchmark—Age Friendly Cities. The checklist that they created is an excellent description of the infrastructure needs of the disabled.[18] For example, New York City has very publicly supported the Age Friendly Cities initiative.[19] This has led to a whole range of initiatives. The authors would like New York City's Metropolitan Transportation Authority

---

17. Theda Radtke, and Pamela Rackow, "Autonomous Motivation Is Not Enough: The Role of Compensatory Health Beliefs for the Readiness to Change Stair and Elevator Use," *International Journal of Environmental Research and Public Health* 11, no. 12 (2014): 12412-2428.

18. "Checklist of Essential Features of Age-Friendly Cities," World Health Organization, 2007, https://www.who.int/ageing/publications/Age_friendly_cities_checklist.pdf.

19. "Age Friendly NYC: New Commitments for a City for All Ages," Age Friendly NYC, 2017, https://www1.nyc.gov/assets/dfta/downloads/pdf/publications/AgeFriendlyNYC2017.pdf.

(MTA) to fund dramatic accessibility upgrades to the public transportation system. This would meet the needs of the aging population as well as the disabled.

On the international stage, besides the WHO initiative, there is the Convention on the Rights of Persons with Disabilities (CRPD).[20] This has not been ratified by the United States Senate yet. One way to approach it is to begin with the UN booklet that explains the CRPD in basic terms.[21] This is a major civil rights document for the disabled. It is a reminder that there is a need to protect the disabled, many of whom are vulnerable. The authors firmly believe that the United States Senate should ratify it.

What Can Librarians Do?

In conversations with disabled library workers and allies, the topic of job ads came up. As has been previously mentioned, this also came up in the literature.[22] If the reader creates an advertisement for a job at their institution, they should think carefully about advertised requirements for open positions. Has the job ad been reviewed by somebody who doesn't know library jargon? Is a driver's license truly required, or is there a work around? Is it necessary for this person to push

---

20. "Convention on the Rights of Persons with Disabilities," United Nations Department of Economic and Social Affairs, https://www.un.org/development/desa/disabilities/convention-on-the-rights-of-persons-with-disabilities.html.

21. "It's About Ability—An Explanation of the Convention on the Rights of Persons with Disabilities," UNICEF, accessed January 14, 2020. https://www.unicef.org/publications/index_43893.html.

22.Rita Thomas Noel, "Employing the Disabled: A How and Why Approach," *Training and Development Journal* 44, no. 8 (1990): 26-32.

full book carts? Is travel around your library system truly required? Can some of the meetings be virtual? Can your library system offer transportation between branches? We need to think creatively. The pay-off is broadening your pool of candidates, accessing talented professionals who will make a commitment to your organization.

We all want to be seen as valuable workers and treated equally. All workers want their strengths acknowledged. Throughout the interviews there was a plea for the fostering of a culture of empathy (See Resources for suggested readings).

Along with empathy, we also heard a lot about fostering communication. One must be aware that communication has a lot of moving parts. Discussing communication problems with persons with cognitive issues was very eye-opening. We heard about the need to offer written instructions, if spoken instructions are not able to be followed. So much of what we take for granted needs to be more flexible. Society should be more aware that a visually impaired person may be missing nonverbal cues.

We need help building community. While interviewing it became very clear that our interviewees wanted to be able to talk to each other. The authors are working on forming a Google Group to give people a chance to make connections, but it is harder than we thought. We need to learn from other under-represented groups. Building supportive networks is critically important.[23] Brown and Sheidlower think there should be meetings of the disabled at conferences. There are many possibilities, including virtual conferences. Please

---

23. Anantachai et al., "Establishing a Communal Network."

contact the authors if you have suggestions to expand this effort.

Community can also be local. Our experience has been that the issues that are raised by this research have a local community. It takes time, but the rewards can be tremendous. We are not alone. Because we both work for the City University of New York (CUNY), we have had the opportunity to offer a Disability Services Roundtable through the Library Association of the City University of New York (LACUNY). One does not have to be disabled to take part; you must only have a passion for serving disabled library patrons.

It is necessary to recognize that you are part of the solution. One of the important insights in the literature is that libraries are not neutral. Gibson et al. urge libraries to consider deeply the needs of their communities.[24] Drabinski points out that "as users interact with these structures to browse and retrieve materials, they inevitably learn negative stereotypes about race, gender, class and other social identities."[25] Guevera provides an excellent list of resources under the heading of "starting the conversation."[26]

The work of an individual to affirm this research begins with understanding that "functional variation" is all around

24. Amelia N. Gibson, Renate L. Chancellor, Nicole A. Cooke, Sarah Park Dahlen, Shari A. Lee, and Yasmeen L. Shorish, "Libraries on the Frontlines: Neutrality and Social Justice," *Equality, Diversity and Inclusion: An International Journal* 36, no. 8 (2017): 751-766.

25. Emily Drabinski, "Queering the Catalog: Queer Theory and the Politics of Correction," *Library Quarterly* 83, no. 2 (2013): 97

26. Senovia Guevara, "Starting the Conversation: The Disabled Library Patron," *Information Outlook (Online)* 22, no. 6 (2018): 6-15.

us. Make no assumptions about anyone's ability based on first impressions. If you teach, learn everything you can about inclusive instruction (see chapter 9 for inclusive instruction).

What Can Library Associations Do?
This research has highlighted the importance of understanding the growing diversity of the profession. The American Library Association has committed itself to equity, diversity, and inclusion.[27] Diversity Counts, which was a study done by the American Library Association in 2006 and 2012, needs to be expanded and redone every two years.[28] It needs to be done more frequently so that we can make changes and see progress.

One interesting idea that we would like to explore is the impact of virtual conferences. There are librarians with disabilities at library conferences, but many will benefit from not having to travel. How can we make a virtual conference as worthwhile as a face-to-face conference?

There is a real need to integrate issues of equity, diversity, and inclusion into the library school curriculum, and to include disability studies as an important layer to that initiative. One of the most important takeaways from this study is the understanding that equity, diversity, and inclusion needs to include the disabled, and that the disabled need to stand with anyone else who is being discriminated against.

---

27. "Equity, Diversity, and Inclusion," American Library Association, accessed January 14, 2020, http://www.ala.org/advocacy/diversity.

28. "Diversity Counts," American Library Association, accessed April 7, 2020, http://www.ala.org/aboutala/offices/diversity/diversitycounts/divcounts.

A Tragedy

Malaysia Goodson came into New York City from her home in Stamford, Connecticut, to do some shopping. She brought her one-year-old along in a stroller. She fell and died while trying to take the stroller down a flight of stairs at a subway station that had no elevator.[1] Her death sparked a major conversation about accessibility issues with New York City subways.[2] It stressed a common cause that the disabled have with young parents, as well as anyone who is carrying bundles.

1. Gold and Fizsimmons.

2. James Barron, "'We All Need to Help': Outrage and Empathy After a Mother's Death on Subway Stairs," *New York Times*, January 30, 2019, https://nyti.ms/2SeCC4V.

Stairs

Thinking about stairs, and how they connect to privilege: Could you navigate through your life as it is now, if you were in a wheelchair? As has been discussed in the advocacy section, it's not just about wheelchairs. Elevators are needed by everybody.

So how do buildings get built today that ignore Universal Design? One of the most challenging designs is the new Hunter's Point Library in the Queens Public Library system.[1] The architect's explanation is disingenuous. The design was set before we knew how important accessibility is. How do we integrate Universal Design into buildings that are currently being designed?

On the other hand, there are historical artifacts. "There are 64 step streets in the Bronx."[2] Thought experiment: How long will older pieces of infrastructure be ignored?

---

1. Sharon Otterman, "New Library Is a $41.5 Million Masterpiece. But About Those Stairs," *New York Times*, November 5, 2019, https://nyti.ms/2oNmWZT.

2. Ian Michaels and Alana Morales, "City Completes Reconstruction of Clifford Place Step Street in Morris Heights," New York City Department of Design and Construction, August, 28,2019, https://www1.nyc.gov/site/ddc/about/press-releases/2019/pr-082819-Reconstruction-Clifford-Place-Step-Street.page.

12. LIFE WRITING

Life writing is a thriving genre in disability studies.[1] Many authors feel called to bear witness to their process, and to educate both the disabled and the able-bodied. This begins with accepting that individual voices are worth considering. "Personal problems are political problems."[2]

Nancy Mairs reflects on the writing process: "All writers, it occurs to me, may be driven to their desks less by creative genius than by the desire to produce the book they would most like to read."[3] She does own that while this is probably true for all writers, it has particular resonance when walking what feels like a unique path. G. Thomas Crouser suggests that, "Whatever form it takes, bodily dysfunction tends to heighten consciousness of self and of contingency."[4] Crouser chronicles the proliferation of multiple forms of disability memoirs in the recent decades.[5]

---

1. G. Thomas Couser and Susannah B. Mintz, *Disability Experiences: Memoirs, Autobiographies, and Other Personal Narratives* (Farmington Hills, MI: Macmillan, 2019).

2. Hamish, "Personal," 4

3. Nancy Mairs, "Forward," in *Recovering Bodies: Illness, Disability, and Life-Writing,* by G. Thomas Crouser, (Madison, WI: University of Wisconsin Press, 1997), x.

4. G. Thomas Crouser, *Recovering Bodies: Illness, Disability, and Life-Writing* (Madison, WI: University of Wisconsin Press, 1997), 5.

5. G. Thomas Crouser, "Introduction: Disability and Life Writing," *Journal of Literacy & Cultural Disability Studies* 5, no. 3 (2011), 229.

The range of experiences and insights within the disabled community is varied. The best way to demonstrate this is to let disabled library workers speak for themselves. The authors decided to seek narratives from this community; what follows is a range of these voices.

Chronic Condition

Something I want my managers and supervisors to know about having a disability—especially an invisible one—is that sometimes I really do need help, and asking for it is hard. The need to prove myself, to pull my own weight, to not let others down or be a burden, to not seem incapable or flaky or unreliable; everyone has that fear at work, but when you have a disability, it is a constant presence in your work life, and can be developed enough almost to the point of a phobia. I'm constantly worrying about how others perceive me as a co-worker, and it is exhausting. It can also mean I delay asking for help too long or struggle with asking when I finally do. In other parts of my life, I might be better at admitting difficulty or an inability to do something, but the culture of work in the United States is such a total indoctrination that even if I can manage the difficult skill of seeking support outside of work, doing the same thing at work can be almost terrifying. And we all, disabled or not, have heard horror stories about working while ill or disabled; everyone is aware of them and how they aren't really infrequent enough to truly be considered an anomaly, so if you live with a chronic condition, the very legitimate threat of losing a job or being subject to a hostile workplace is always in the back of your mind. It means we get a little neurotic about needing to prove ourselves. Please understand that; please don't take advantage of it; and please know that by the time I'm asking for help, I don't do it lightly and I need you to take it seriously, because I really do feel like my back is against a wall.

Authors' Observation:

- Fear of being discriminated against is very real.

Hearing Impairment

"Seeking to understand" could be the motto of my life with hearing impairment. I work in the public services department at a large university library—interacting with students and faculty is the core of my job. Over the past twenty years, as my hearing has gotten worse, that interaction has been fraught with frustration for both me and whoever is trying to get me to understand. I mishear things constantly—once I freaked out when I heard someone say, "And I know I'm a cannibal" (she actually said, "And I know I'm accountable"). I've missed meetings because I didn't hear some change in time or place that was spoken aloud but not conveyed in writing. For me, spoken words are like smoke rings—they dissipate even as they appear and quickly lose their resolution.

I am grateful to the university for the multiple accommodations made to help me do my job. I now do research assistance and the reference desk with a student assistant who repeats what people are asking. I also have a special phone in my office and a Roger Pen for meetings. The technology and the student assistants are helpful, but there are three things that would help me even more:

1. For the presenters at every meeting of 10+ people I'm required to attend, to use amplification.
2. For people to remember to make a few small alterations in their volume and style when speaking to me.
3. For every important communication to be in writing.

My disability is invisible, so in order to get someone to help me, I must disclose my problem, which alters the tone of the interaction. When I say I'm hearing impaired, some raise their voice volume to a startling level—usually I prevent this by explaining that all I need is for them to speak more slowly and do so while facing me. Everyone cooperates for about ten minutes and then most go back to their default style. I do understand why—I used to do it myself years ago when dealing with hearing-impaired family members who had the same inherited problem I do.

Every verbal interaction in my workplace is a challenge as I daily seek to understand what my colleagues and the library's patrons are saying. I want to understand, of course, but most of the time that requires multiple takes. The progress of my hearing deterioration is slow, but it has gone down steadily since I was a teenager. Now, at age sixty, I wonder if I'll be able to hear well enough to work the next seven-to-ten years, as my bank account tells me I must do.

Authors' Observation:

- Aging with a progressive disability can be deeply challenging.

Library Director

When I finally landed in public libraries, it was as if I'd come home. I'd worked as a tutor and a researcher prior to working in a library and both jobs were less physical than library work. I have a minor case of Cerebral Palsy, which affects my gait and fine motor use of my left hand primarily. I found my job as the circulation desk of an urban library challenging and slightly embarrassing as I didn't like my disability on display (and it was every time I tried to do with one hand what another person might do with two). However, my co-workers and the patrons were understanding and I grew more comfortable during my time on the circulation desk.

I was good at my job, and received three promotions in four years. After I received my MLIS I was offered the position of Director of a small public library. After several years of rallying the community, we were able to build the first independent library facility in the history of the town. And during that time, I became nationally known as one of the first proponents of graphic novels in public libraries. In addition, I published a few books on graphic novel collection development. I became more ambitious and sought positions in bigger libraries. I went on eighteen [job] interviews in thirteen years. Most seemed to go well, but they rarely resulted in job offers, although I was a finalist several times. The only explanation that made sense to me was that my left hand, which sometimes experienced spasms when I was nervous, was the subject of alarmed looks and occasional stares during the interviews.

Authors' Observation:

- Disabled librarians can be highly qualified profess-ionals. It sounds as if this respondent has been a victim of ableism.

Post-Traumatic Stress Disorder (PTSD)

I graduated with my MLS in May of 2019. Prior to library school, I had been diagnosed with complex PTSD from a previous career in public service as a 911 dispatcher. I knew that when I graduated, finding a position and dealing with my diagnosis would not be easy, but I was willing to put in the work to do it. I started subbing for a large library system about an hour and a half from where I live and was lucky enough to land a full-time role with them as an Adult Services

Librarian in one of their smaller branches only a month after my official degree conferral. I was so excited to be able to start my full-time library career, but also nervous because my social skills and day-to-day life were still a bit of a wreck. I have a hard time trusting people and letting them in. I have anxiety over the craziest things. I have more "off" feeling days than normal ones.

I didn't want to hide my struggle in this position because my manager had a background in psychology, and I felt safe confiding in her. We had a decent relationship for several months until I had my first rough patch. The weather was starting to get colder, I had bad anniversary dates coming up, and our branch was in a negative mood from lots of upper management changes. All of this had been too much to deal with, so I called out of work for a couple of days and when I went back, I had to sit down and explain myself. That meeting was a total disaster and I felt ganged up on by my superiors.

From that point on, the relationship with my supervisor drastically changed. She avoided me when she could. She micromanaged me other times. She wouldn't let me participate or take on new tasks without hesitation or being involved. Then, only a few months later when I became eligible for FMLA leave and tried to have a conversation with her about applying for it to have a safety net, she turned the tables on me, blaming me for her anxiety as a supervisor because I could call out at any moment. She also went on to tell me how I wasn't pulling my weight on the team, when she wasn't letting me.

That was my line in the sand. I could take being avoided and I dealt with her micromanaging the best I could, but I would not be talked to that way. I've worked too hard to overcome the struggles that come with my mental illness.

I walked away from that position by only giving a few days' notice and requesting no contact with my immediate supervisor while I finished up my work. I don't regret my decision, because I couldn't stay in a job that wasn't safe or healthy. I put my recovery first, which is what I hope to inspire others to do as well.

Authors' Observation:

- We all have a right to be treated with respect.

Sensory Overload and the Autistic Librarian

Most students and academic librarians are familiar with the experience of "library anxiety"—that is, the feeling of a library being overwhelming for someone who is new to it and needing to navigate it independently for the first time. The lights, the new website and a new search engine, even the new furniture and shelving arrangements can add up to making the average student very anxious.

This sensation is intensified for those of us on the spectrum. Many people with neurodevelopmental disorders, like autism and ADHD, experience something called "sensory overload" at a much lower threshold than those who do not have a neurodevelopmental disability. This means that the noise of students talking, the buzz and the intensity of fluorescent lights, and the non-intuitive navigability of a website can make us shut down or make us have serious anxiety, and as a result it might mean that we avoid the library entirely. Even if the library is chock full of resources for students, if the library is inadvertently hostile to students with disabilities, that means that those students will avoid the library—and its resources—and not get the kind of support that their classmates who don't have autism or ADHD might be getting.

For example, I have both autism and ADHD. The library was the most frequented spot on my campus, but because the library wasn't quiet and because of how the library was lit, it meant that I couldn't consistently use the space without risking burning myself out even more than I already was. As a result, I had to do most of my work by myself, confined to my dorm room. I would come to the library to help patrons, but I could not ever use the library for studying or communal gatherings.

This meant several things:

- First, I wasn't able to do research at the library and use research materials and services consistently like my classmates, which meant I had to pull from external resources that weren't as consistent or as reliable for my academic endeavors.

- Second, since I wasn't able to go to the library out[side] of work hours, I couldn't frequent it as a "third space" and make friends, therefore cordoning me off from my classmates socially due to my disabilities.

- Third, job events were often hosted at the library where students would come in and have their resumes and cover letters looked at by librarians and other professionals to give edits and advice. This—along with other types of events that were similar—meant that since they were [held] in a hostile environment to someone like me, they were not available to me and other people like me who had issues in the space related to sensory overload. Hence, as a student (even while *being employed by the library myself*) I suffered academically, socially, and professionally due to a lack of accessibility measures within the library's inherent structure.

Authors' observation:
- This narrative demonstrates the importance of Universal Design in libraries.

What It's Like Being a Librarian with a Disability

Since I started my career in libraries, I have had many highs and lows related to my disability. I have seen some amazing work done to make libraries more inclusive. I have also experienced unfortunate situations that have made me wonder how far we have really come and how long it might take us to get where we need to be.

Working in libraries with a disability can be wonderful because they are for everyone and have recently become strong advocates for equity, diversity, and inclusion. On a national level, libraries have made significant strides towards being more accommodating. However, even when equity and inclusion are preached inside the walls of some libraries, they are not always practiced, specifically when it comes to serving the needs of their staff with disabilities.

An example is the discrimination and micro-aggressions I consistently faced while working at my first library job. I was infantilized because of my disability and treated as though I should be grateful to so much as have a job even when I outperformed co-workers. This was particularly relevant when I requested a raise and promotion. On one occasion, I applied for a job within the agency that primarily consisted of consulting and advocating for inclusion throughout the state (something I was already doing). In this instance, I was not given an interview and then learned, through co-workers, that the supervisor said it was because they simply could not hire someone like me who could not drive—a perfunctory excuse since I knew the consultants typically went out in pairs. Years later, I was asked to be the Outreach Librarian since I was already doing a significant amount of outreach. Although this job would require much more skilled work than what I was then doing and much more travel, I was not offered a raise nor a reclassification—something typically given to non-disabled staff. Instead, I was told that I would have to "earn" it as if I had not already proven my worth. I was also told that "If [I] thought [I] could do better then [I] should look for a job elsewhere" and that I was "replaceable." It was then that I knew I was never going to be taken seriously, appreciated, or even treated the same way as my co-workers who did not have a disability.

The sad part is, as a person and an employee with a disability, I wish they knew how hard I worked to prove my value to the agency. I consistently excelled to show them I was not only capable but also worthy of my position in hopes of one day moving up within the agency. I created, implemented, and managed large-scale, statewide programs, expanded and improved existing services, and traveled whenever I was asked to do it, even though I was not comfortable with how often they requested me to do so. Even being named an "ALA Emerging Leader" and writing an ASGCLA[6] award-winning nomination for a project I managed was not enough.

I also wish they knew how much I loved the agency and the services we provided to patrons with print disabilities like myself, putting up with things I know now I shouldn't have because of how much I believed in the agency and in them. I thought they could change their minds about people with disabilities if I tried hard enough. Lastly, I wish they realized that having someone with a different perspective was

---

6. Association of Specialized, Government, and Cooperative Library Agencies

a blessing, not a curse, and recognized the opportunities it presented for growth and change.

Authors' Observation:

- Employment discrimination based on disability is as reprehensible as racism. It harms both the agency and the employee.

Things I Wish My Employer Understood about My Disability

As a librarian with a visual impairment, many of my challenges revolve around transportation. I am fortunate enough to have access to public transportation despite living in a small town. However, my housing choices are limited by available bus routes. Public transit also lessens considerably in times when students are off-campus, so I have to consider scenarios such as: how will I travel from home to work in the dead of winter when sidewalks are covered by two feet of snow and buses are not running? My solutions to these problems include: living in student housing, riding my bike to work (cautiously), hiking six miles round trip for groceries, having parents drive me to out-of-town doctors' appointments, catching rides to the airport, and—should I wish to buy anything in the town nine miles to the east—investing two to three hours to ride my bike or begging an occasional ride.

As a librarian with these transportation contingencies, I am grateful that my job provides me with flexible hours and remote work options. I did, however, find this town extremely isolating when I first arrived and wish employers would consider the kinds of barriers small-town life can present for new employees with disabilities. Transportation barriers don't just limit my housing options and daily schedule. They also create distance from coworkers and, for me, helped instigate a certain amount of anxiety and depression. What could my employer have done differently? As an introvert with poor vision, I experienced extreme isolation when I arrived. It would have helped if I had been introduced to others and actively invited into support communities. For a long time, many of my coworkers remained blurry non-entities in my life, and I found it difficult to find friends and community with little external support.

Authors' Observation:

- This is a good insight into what being visually impaired is like, and the barriers imposed by public transit in rural America.

RESOURCES

Recommended Web Resources

Equity, Diversity, and Inclusion
http://www.ala.org/aboutala/offices/diversity/edi
Resources from the American Library Association about the work being done within the association to support equity, diversity and inclusion.

Resources
https://www.asgcladirect.org/resources/
The Association of Specialized Government and Cooperative Library Agencies is the main source of resources for promoting accessibility within ALA.

Anti-Racism Training
People's Institute for Survival and Beyond
https://www.pisab.org/
The People's Institute is a major source of anti-racism training for organizations.

"Universal Access: Making Library Resources Accessible to People with Disabilities." University of Washington
https://www.washington.edu/doit/universal-access-making-library-resources-accessible-people-disabilities.
This is an impressive list of resources from the University of Washington.

The Charter for Compassion
https://charterforcompassion.org/charter
This is a social movement developed by Karen Armstrong. We have included the Charter in the Appendix.

Empathy Lab
https://www.empathylab.uk/
Reading promotes empathy.

Recommended Books

Allen, Madelene Burley. *Listening: The Forgotten Skill.* New York: John Wiley, 1995.
An important basic text for anyone who wants to become a better listener.

Armstrong, Karen. *Twelve Steps to a Compassionate Life.* Toronto: Knopf Canada, 2011.
Karen Armstrong is a very important voice of conscience. This text describes how she founded the Charter for Compassion, and her plan to help everyone become more compassionate.

Kendall, Mikki. *Hood Feminism: Notes from the Women That a Movement Forgot.* New York: Viking, 2020.
This is an impassioned restatement of what feminism can become, if we take seriously the quality of life of all women.

Kendi, Ibram X. *How to Be an Antiracist.* One World/Ballantine, 2019.
An antiracist is a person who is actively engaged in opposing racism wherever it is found. This is a profound challenge, that everyone should consider.

Kowalsky, Michelle, and John Woodruff. *Creating Inclusive Library Environments: A Planning Guide for Serving Patrons with Disabilities.* Chicago: ALA Editions. 2017.
This is a very practical guide, certainly worth considering when libraries go through any form of renovation or reevaluation of services.

Krznaric, Roman. *Empathy: Why it Matters, and How to Get It.* New York: Penguin, 2015.
This is a very thought-provoking text, that outlines what it means to be empathetic. Recommended for anyone who wants to become more empathetic.

VanDuinkerken, Wyoma, and Wendi Arant. *Leading Libraries: How to Create a Service Culture.* Chicago: American Library Association, 2015.
Their central thesis is servant leadership, which they describe as focusing on the needs of the patron.

Worline, Monica, and Jane E. Dutton. *Awakening Compassion at Work: The Quiet Power that Elevates People and Organizations.* Oakland: Berrett-Koehler Publishers, 2017.
Empathy within the context of the workplace. This is an important text for managers.

Zaki, Jamil. *The War for Kindness: Building Empathy in a Fractured World.* New York: Crown 2019.
We are losing touch with each other. Nevertheless, we can learn to grow our empathy.

Recommended Articles

Bruneau, Emile G., Mina Cikara, and Rebecca Saxe. "Parochial Empathy Predicts Reduced Altruism and the Endorsement of Passive Harm." *Social Psychological and Personality Science* 8, no. 8 (2017): 934-942. https://dash.harvard.edu/handle/1/34652051.

Dodell-Feder, David, and Diana I. Tamir. "Fiction Reading Has a Small Positive Impact on Social Cognition: A Meta-Analysis." *Journal of Experimental Psychology: General* 147, no. 11 (2018): 1713-727.

References

Abberley, Paul. "The Concept of Oppression and the Development of a Social Theory of Disability." *Disability, Handicap & Society* 2, no. 1 (March 1987): 5–19.

————. "Work, Utopia and Impairment" In *Disability and Society: Emerging Issues and Insights,* edited by Len Barton, 61-79. London: Longman, 1996.

Acker, Joan, Kate Barry, and Joke Esseveld. "Objectivity and Truth: Problems in Doing Feminist Research." In *Beyond Methodology: Feminist Scholarship as Lived Research,* edited by Mary Margaret Fonow and Judith A. Cook, 133-153. Bloomington, IN: Indiana University Press, 1991.

Alson, Jason K. "Interns or Professionals? A Common Misnomer Applied to Diversity Resident Librarians Can Potentially Degrade and Divide." In *Where Are All the Librarians of Color? The Experiences of People of Color in Academia,* edited by Rebecca Hankins and Miguel Juárez, 71-93. Sacramento, CA: Library Juice Press, 2015.

American Library Association. "Equity, Diversity and Inclusion." Accessed January 14, 2020. http://www.ala.org/advocacy/diversity.

———. "Diversity Counts." Accessed April 7, 2020.
http://www.ala.org/aboutala/offices/diversity/
diversitycounts/divcounts.

Annamma, Subini Ancy, David J. Connor, and Beth
Ferri. "Dis/ability Critical Race Studies (DisCrit):
Theorizing at the Intersections of Race and Dis/
ability." In *DisCrit: Disability Studies and Critical
Race Theory in Education,* edited by David J. Connor,
Beth A. Ferri, and Subini A. Annamma, 9-32. New
York: Teacher's College Press, 2016.

Anantachai, Tarida, Latrice Booker, Althea Lazzaro, and
Martha Parker. "Establishing a Communal Network
for Professional Advancement among Librarians of
Color." In *Where Are All the Librarians of Color? The
Experiences of People of Color in Academia,* edited
by Rebecca Hankins and Miguel Juárez, 31-53.
Sacramento, CA: Library Juice Press, 2015.

Appleby, Yvon. "Out in the Margins." *Disability and
Society* 9, no. 1 (1994): 19-32.

Artiles, Alfredo J. "Untangling the Racialization of
Disabilities: An Intersectionality Critique Across
Disability Models." *Du Bois Review: Social Science
Research on Race* 10, no. 2 (2013): 329-347.

Asch, Adrienne. "Critical Race Theory, Feminism, and
Disability: Reflections on Social Justice and Personal
Identity." *Ohio State Law Journal* 62 (2001): 391-423.

Barnes, Colin. "Disability, the Organization of Work,
and the Need for Change." Statement presented

to the Organisation for Economic Co-operation and Development Conference "Transforming Disability into Ability," March 6, 2003. http://www.independentliving.org/docs6/barnes20030306.html.

Barron, James. "'We All Need to Help': Outrage and Empathy After a Mother's Death on Subway Stairs." *New York Times,* January 30, 2019. https://nyti.ms/2SeCC4V.

Barton, Len. "Sociology and Disability: Some Emerging Issues." In *Disability and Society Emerging Issues and Insights,* edited by Len Barton, 3-17. London: Longman,1996.

Begum, Nasa. "Disabled Women and the Feminist Agenda." *Feminist Review* 40, no. 1 (1992): 70-84.

Bell, Chris. "Is Disability Studies Actually White Disability Studies?" In *The Disability Studies Reader*, 5th ed., edited by Lennard Davis, 404- 415. New York: Routledge: 2017.

Berg, Paula, "Ill/Legal: The Meaning and Function of the Category of Disability in Antidiscrimination Law." *CUNY Academic Works*, 1999. https://academicworks.cuny.edu/cl_pubs/276.

Berger, Ronald J. *Introducing Disability Studies*. Boulder, CO: Lynne Rienner Publishers, 2013.

Bhargava, Saurabh, and George Loewenstein. "Choosing a Health Insurance Plan: Complexity and Consequences." *JAMA* 314, no. 23 (2015): 2505-506.

Bickenbach, Jerome, Christine Bigby, Luis Salvador-
    Carulla, Tamar Heller, Matilde Leonardi, Barbara
    LeRoy, Jennifer Mendez, Michelle Putnam, and
    Andria Spindel. "The Toronto Declaration on
    Bridging Knowledge, Policy and Practice in Aging
    and Disability: Toronto, Canada, March 30, 2012."
    International Journal of Integrated Care 12 (2012).

Bordo, Susan. *Unbearable Weight: Feminism, Western
    Culture, and the Body.* Berkeley, CA: University of
    California Press, 2004.

Brook, Freeda, Dave Ellenwood, and Althea Eannace
    Lazzaro. "In Pursuit of Antiracist Social Justice:
    Denaturalizing Whiteness in the Academic Library."
    Library Trends 64, no. 2 (2015): 246-284.

Brown, Mary E. "Invisible Debility: Attitudes Toward the
    Underrepresented in Library Workplaces." *Public
    Library Quarterly* 34, no. 2 (2015): 124-133.

Brown, Robin. "Passing." *The Adventures of a Three Wheeled
    Librarian.* (2018). http://threewheeledlibrarian.
    weebly.com/adventures-of-a-three-wheeled-librarian/
    passing2842796.

Brown, Robin, and Scott Sheidlower. "Claiming Our Space:
    A Quantitative and Qualitative Picture of Disabled
    Librarians." *Library Trends* 67, no. 3 (2019): 471-486.
    https://academicworks.cuny.edu/bm_pubs/115/.

Brune, Jeffrey A., and Daniel J. Wilson. *Disability and
    Passing: Blurring the Lines of Identity.* Philadelphia:
    Temple University Press, 2013.

Butler, Judith. *Gender Trouble: Feminism and the Subversion of Identity*. New York: Routledge, 1999.

Cameron, Colin. "Further Towards an Affirmation Model." In *Disability Studies: Emerging Insights and Perspectives*, edited by Thomas Campbell, 14-30. Leeds, UK: Disability Press, 2008.

Carpenter, Scott. "The Americans with Disabilities Act: Accommodation in Ohio." *College and Research Libraries* 57 no. 6 (1996): 555-566. https://crl.acrl.org/index.php/crl/issue/view/948.

Center for Applied Special Technology (CAST). "Universal Design for Learning Guidelines." Version 2.2, 2018. http://udlguidelines.cast.org.

Clair, Judith A., Joy E. Beatty, and Tammy L. MacLean. "Out of Sight but Not Out of Mind: Managing Invisible Social Identities in the Workplace." *Academy of Management Review* 30, no. 1 (2005): 78-95.

Clare, Eli. *Exile and Pride: Disability, Queerness, and Liberation*. Durham, NC: Duke University Press, 2015.

Collins, Patricia Hill. *Black Feminist Thought: Knowledge, Consciousness, and the Politics of Empowerment*. 2nd ed. New York: Routledge, 2000.

Collins, Patricia Hill, and Sirma Bilge. *Intersectionality*. Cambridge, UK: Polity Press, 2016.

Cook, Samantha, and Kristina Clement. "Navigating the Hidden Void: The Unique Challenges of

Accommodating Library Employees with Invisible Disabilities." *Journal of Academic Librarianship* 45, no. 5 (2019): 1.

Corbett, Jenny. "A Proud Label: Exploring the Relationship Between Disability Politics and Gay Pride." *Disability & Society* 9, no. 3 (1994): 343-357.

Crabbe, Megan Jayne. *Body Positive Power.* London: Vermillion. 2018.

Crenshaw, Kimberlé. "Mapping the Margins: Intersectionality, Identity Politics, and Violence Against Women of Color." *Stanford Law Review* 43 (1990): 1241-1299.

Cresswell, Stephen. "The Last Days of Jim Crow in Southern Libraries." *Libraries & Culture* (1996): 557-573.

Crouser, G. Thomas. "Introduction: Disability and Life Writing," *Journal of Literacy & Cultural Disability Studies* 5, no. 3 (2011), 229-241.

———. *Recovering Bodies: Illness, Disability, and Life Writing.* Madison, WI: University of Wisconsin Press, 1997.

———, and Susannah B. Mintz. *Disability Experiences: Memoirs, Autobiographies, and Other Personal Narratives.* Farmington Hills, MI: Macmillan, 2019.

Davies, Kim. "A Troubled Identity: Putting Butler to Work on the Comings and Goings of Asperger's Syndrome." In *Disability Studies: Educating for Inclusion,* edited. by Tim Corcoran, Julie White, and Ben Whitburn, 195-214. Boston: Sense Publishers, 2015.

Dewey, Barbara I. "The Imperative for Diversity: ARL's Progress and Role." *portal: Libraries and the Academy* 9, no. 3 (2009): 355-361.

Drabinski, Emily. "Queering the Catalog: Queer Theory and the Politics of Correction." *Library Quarterly* 83, no. 2 (2013): 94-111.

Davis, Lennard J. *Enforcing Normalcy: Disability, Deafness, and the Body.* New York: Verso, 1995.

Davis, N. Ann. "Invisible Disability." *Ethics* 116, no. 1 (2005): 153-213.

DiAngelo, Robin. "White Fragility." International Journal of Critical Pedagogy 3, no. 3 (2011): 54-70. http://libjournal.uncg.edu/ijcp/article/view/249/116.

Dow, Mirah Jane, Brady D. Lund, and William K. Douthit. "Investigating the Link between Unemployment and Disability." *International Journal of Information, Diversity, & Inclusion (IJIDI)* 4, no. 1 (2020). https://jps.library.utoronto.ca/index.php/ijidi/index

Dykstra, Natalie A. "'Trying to Idle': Work and Disability in the Diary of Alice James." In *The New Disability History: American Perspectives,* edited by Paul K. Longmore, and Lauri Umansky, 107-130. New York: New York University Press, 2001.

Erevelles, Nirmala, and Andrea Minear. "Unspeakable Offenses: Untangling Race and Disability in

Discourses of Intersectionality." *Journal of Literary & Cultural Disability Studies* 4, no. 2 (2010): 127-145. https://doi.org/10.3828/jlcds.2010.11.

Finch, Janet. "Community Care: Developing Non-Sexist Alternatives." *Critical Social Policy* 3, no. 9 (1983): 6-18.

Flink, Patrick J. "Invisible Disabilities, Stigma, and Student Veterans: Contextualizing the Transition to Higher Education." *Journal of Veterans Studies* 2, no. 2 (2017): 110-120. https://journal-veterans-studies.org/.

Gallo, Marcia M. "To Barbara Gittings, 1932-2007: Thank You." *Gay & Lesbian Review Worldwide*, May, (2007), 7-8.

Garland Thomson, Rosemarie. *Extraordinary Bodies: Figuring Physical Disability in American Culture and Literature.* New York: Columbia University Press, 2017.

———. "Integrating Disability, Transforming Feminist Theory," In *Feminist Disability Studies,* edited by Kim Q. Hall, 13-47. Bloomington, IN: Indiana University Press, 2011.

Gibson, Amelia N., Renate L. Chancellor, Nicole A. Cooke, Sarah Park Dahlen, Shari A. Lee, and Yasmeen L. Shorish. "Libraries on the Frontlines: Neutrality and Social Justice." *Equality, Diversity and Inclusion: An International Journal* 36, no. 8 (2017): 751-766.

Goffman, Erving. *Stigma: Notes on the Management of Spoiled Identity.* New York: Simon and Schuster, 1963.

Gold, Michael, and Emma G. Fitzsimmons. "Young Mother, Hauling Child and Stroller Down Subway Steps, Dies." *New York Times*, January 30, 2019.

Gordon, Lewis R. "White Privilege and the Problem with Affirmative Action." In *"I Don't See Color": Personal and Critical Perspectives on White Privilege,* edited by Bettina Bergo and Tracey Nicholls, 27-39. University Park, PA: Pennsylvania State University Press, 2015.

Grim, Andrew. "Sitting-In for Disability Rights: The Section 504 Protests of the 1970s." *O Say Can You See: Stories from the Museum,* July 8, 2015. https://americanhistory.si.edu/blog/sitting-disability-rights-section-504-protests-1970s.

Grue, Jan. "The Social Meaning of Disability: A Reflection on Categorisation, Stigma and Identity." *Sociology of Health and Illness* 38, no. 6 (2016): 957-964.

Guevara, Senovia. "Starting the Conversation: The Disabled Library Patron," *Information Outlook (Online)* 22, no. 6 (2018): 6-15.

Hanisch, Carol. "The Personal is Political." (1969). http://www.carolhanisch.org/CHwritings/PersonalIsPol.pdf.

Hankins, Rebecca. "Racial Realism or Foolish Optimism: An African American Muslim Woman in the

Field." In *Where Are All the Librarians of Color? The Experiences of People of Color in Academia,* edited by Rebecca Hankins and Miguel Juárez, 209-219. Sacramento, CA: Library Juice Press, 2015.

Hartsell-Gundy, Arianne, Jessica Hernández, Ed Garcia, JP Porcaro, and Jennifer Wann Walker. "Emerging Leaders Project F: ASCLA 21st Century Grant." 2010. Accessed December 16, 2019. https://connect.ala.org/communities/community-home/librarydocuments/viewdocument?DocumentKey=CCC8C59B-D0DC-446B-B237-C89CEFFD404C.

Jans, Lita H., H. Stephen Kaye, and Erica C. Jones. "Getting Hired: Successfully Employed People with Disabilities Offer Advice on Disclosure, Interviewing, and Job Search." *Journal of Occupational Rehabilitation* 22, no. 2 (2012): 155-165.

Kattari, Shanna K., Miranda Olzman, and Michele D. Hanna. "'You Look Fine!' Ableist Experiences by People with Invisible Disabilities." *Affilia* 33, no. 4 (2018): 477-492.

Kendall, Mikki. *Hood Feminism: Notes from the Women That a Movement Forgot.* New York: Viking, 2020.

Kendi, Ibram X. *How to Be an Antiracist.* New York: One World, 2019.

Klein, Bonnie Sherr. "'We Are Who You Are': Feminism and Disability." *Ms.* 3, no. 3 (1992):70-74.

Kumbier, Alana, and Julia Starkey. "Access Is Not Problem Solving: Disability Justice and Libraries." *Library Trends* 64, no. 3 (2016): 468-491.

Lebrecht, James and Nicole Newnham. *Crip Camp: A Disability Revolution.* Hollywood, CA: Higher Ground Productions, 2020.

Letnikova, Galina. "LILAC: Planted at CUNY Ten Years Ago and Still Blooming." *LACUNY News* 33, no. 2 (2014). https://academicworks.cuny.edu/lg_pubs/46.

Lewis, Jill. "Information Equality for Individuals with Disabilities: Does It Exist?" *Library Quarterly* 83, no. 3 (2013): 229-235.

Lewin, Tamar. "Disabled Woman's Care Given to Lesbian Partner." *New York Times,* Dec 18, 1991.

Link, Bruce G., and Jo C. Phelan. "Conceptualizing Stigma." *Annual Review of Sociology* 27, no. 1 (2001): 363-385.

Linton, Simi. *Claiming Disability: Knowledge and Identity.* New York: New York University Press, 1998.

Lorde, Audre. "Age, Race, Class, and Sex: Women Redefining Difference." In *Sister Outsider.* Freedom, CA: Crossing Press, 2007.

Mairs, Nancy. "Forward." In *Recovering Bodies: Illness, Disability, and Life-Writing,* G. Thomas Couser, p. ix-xiii. Madison, WI: University of Wisconsin Press, 1997.

Martinez, Larry R., Katina B. Sawyer, Christian N.
Thoroughgood, Enrica N. Ruggs, and Nicholas
A. Smith. "The Importance of Being 'Me': The
Relation Between Authentic Identity Expression and
Transgender Employees' Work-Related Attitudes and
Experiences." *Journal of Applied Psychology* 102, no. 2
(2017): 215-226.

McIntosh, Peggy. *On Privilege, Fraudulence, and Teaching
as Learning Selected Essays 1981-2019.* New York:
Routledge, 2020.

McRuer, Robert. *Crip Theory: Cultural Signs of Queerness
and Disability.* New York: New York University
Press, 2006.

Michaels, Ian, and Alana Morales. "City Completes
Reconstruction of Clifford Place Step Street in
Morris Heights." New York City Department of
Design and Construction. August, 28,2019. https://
www1.nyc.gov/site/ddc/about/press-releases/2019/
pr-082819-Reconstruction-Clifford-Place-Step-
Street.page.

The Minnesota Governor's Council on Developmental
Disabilities. "The ADA Legacy Project: Moments
in Disability History 27." Minnesota Governor's
Council on Developmental Disabilities, 2020.
https://mn.gov/mnddc/ada-legacy/ada-legacy-
moment27.html.

Moore, Alanna, and Jan Estrellado. "Identity, Activism, Self-
Care, and Women of Color Librarians." In *Pushing
the Margin: Women of Color and Intersectionality in*

LIS, edited by Rose. L. Chou, and Annie Pho, 349-389. Sacramento, CA: Litwin Books, 2018.

Morales, Myrna, Em Claire Knowles, and Chris Bourg. "Diversity, Social Justice, and the Future of Libraries." *portal: Libraries and The Academy* 14, no. 3 (2014): 439-451.

Morris, Jenny. *Pride Against Prejudice: A Personal Politics of Disability.* London: Women's Press, 1991.

National Education Association. "Understanding Universal Design in the Classroom" Accessed January 23,2020. http://www.nea.org/home/34693.htm

Nielsen, Kim. *A Disability History of the United States.* Boston: Beacon Press, 2012.

————. "Helen Keller and the Politics of Civic Fitness." In *The New Disability History: American Perspectives,* edited by Paul K. Longmore and Lauri Umansky. 268-290. New York: New York University Press, 2001.

Noel, Rita Thomas. "Employing the Disabled: A How and Why Approach." *Training and Development Journal* 44, no. 8 (1990): 26-32.

O'Brien, Ruth. *Crippled Justice: The History of Modern Disability Policy in the Workplace.* Chicago: University of Chicago Press, 2001.

Oliver, Mike. "Social Policy and Disability: The Creation of Dependency," *Tidskrift För Rättssociologi* 5, no. 1

(1988): 31-47. https://pdfs.semanticscholar.org/060e/
df5eaf475468e2a89da369be6e2afce3495e.pdf.

Oliver, Michael, and Colin Barnes. *The New Politics of Disablement.* New York: Palgrave MacMillian, 2012.

O'Neill, Anne-Marie, and Christine Urquhart. "Accommodating Employees with Disabilities: Perceptions of Irish Academic Library Managers." *New Review of Academic Librarianship* 17, no. 2 (2011): 234-258.

OToole, Corbett Joan. *Fading Scars: My Queer Disability History.* 2nd ed. Berkeley, CA: Reclamation Press, 2019.

Otterman, Sharon. "New Library Is a $41.5 Million Masterpiece. But About Those Stairs." *New York Times,* November 5, 2019. https://nyti.ms/2oNmWZT.

Oud, Joanne. "Academic Librarians with Disabilities: Job Perceptions and Factors Influencing Positive Workplace Experiences." *Partnership: The Canadian Journal of Library and Information Practice and Research* 13, no. 1 (2018). https://journal.lib.uoguelph.ca/index.php/perj/

Pastrana, Jr., Antonio. "Privileging Oppression: Contradictions in Intersectional Politics." *Western Journal of Black Studies* 34, no. 1 (2010): 53-63.

"Persons with a Disability: Labor Force Characteristics — 2018." *Economic News Release: Persons with a Disability: Labor Force Characteristics.* US Department of Labor, Bureau of Labor Statistics, February 26, 2019. https://www.bls.gov/news.release/pdf/disabl.pdf.

Pionke, J. J. "Toward Holistic Accessibility: Narratives from Functionally Diverse Patrons." *Reference & User Services Quarterly* 57, no. 1 (Fall 2017), 48-56.

———. "Beyond ADA Compliance: The Library as a Place for all." *Urban Library Journal* 23, no. 1 (2017): 3. https://academicworks.cuny.edu/ulj/vol23/iss1/.

Polger, Mark Aaron, and Scott Sheidlower. *Engaging Diverse Learners: Teaching Strategies for Academic Librarians.* Santa Barbara, CA: Libraries Unlimited, 2017.

Radtke, Theda, and Pamela Rackow. "Autonomous Motivation Is Not Enough: The Role of Compensatory Health Beliefs for the Readiness to Change Stair and Elevator Use." *International Journal of Environmental Research and Public Health* 11, no. 12 (2014): 12412-2428. https://www.mdpi.com/journal/ijerph.

Remy, Charlie, and Priscilla Seaman. "Evolving from Disability to Diversity: How to Better Serve High-Functioning Autistic Students." *Reference & User Services Quarterly* 54, no. 1 (2014): 24-28.

Rise and Resist. "Rise and Resist: Elevator Action Group." Accessed January 31, 2020. https://www.riseandresist.org/elevator-action-group.

Roberts, Dorothy. *Fatal Invention: How Science, Politics, and Big Business Re-Create Race in the Twenty-First Century.* New York: The New Press, 2011.

Roulstone, Alan. "Disabled People, Work and Employment: A Global Perspective." In *Routledge Handbook of Disability Studies,* edited by Nick Watson, Carol Thomas, and Alan Roulstone. 222-235. New York: Routledge, 2013.

Rosenberg, Eli. "New York City's Subway System Violates Local and Federal Laws, Disability Groups Say." *New York Times,* April 25, 2017.

Ruiz, Jason. "The Violence of Assimilation: An Interview with Mattilda aka Matt Bernstein Sycamore." *Radical History Review* 100 (2008): 237-247.

Russell, Marta. *Beyond Ramps: Disability at the End of the Social Contract: A Warning from an Uppity Crip.* Monroe, ME: Common Courage Press, 1998.

Sack, Kevin. "Research Finds Wide Disparities in Health Care by Race and Region." *New York Times,* June 5, 2008: A18 (L).

Scambler, Graham, and Anthony Hopkins. "Being Epileptic: Coming to Terms with Stigma." *Sociology of Health and Illness* 8, no. 1 (1986): 26-43.

Schomberg, Jessica. "Disability at Work: Libraries, Built to Exclude." In *The Politics and Theory of Critical Librarianship,* edited by Karen P. Nicholson and

Maura Seale, 111-123. Sacramento, CA: Library Juice Press, 2018.

Schriner, Kay. "A Disability Studies Perspective on Employment Issues and Policies for Disabled People: An International View." In *Handbook of Disability Studies*, edited by Albrecht, Gary L., Katherine D. Seelman, and Michael Bury, 642-662.Thousand Oaks, CA: Sage Publications, 2001.

Scotch, Richard K., and Kay Schriner. "Disability as Human Variation: Implications for Policy." *The Annals of the American Academy of Political and Social Science* 549, No. 1 (1997): 148-159.

Shakespeare, Tom. *Help: Imagining Welfare*. Birmingham, UK: Venture Press, 2000.

———. *Disability Rights and Wrongs Revisited*. London: Routledge, 2014.

Shapiro, Joseph P. *No Pity: People with Disabilities Forging a New Civil Rights Movement*. New York: Three Rivers Press, 1994.

Sheidlower, Scott. "Accommodating the Disabled in Library One-Shots at York College/CUNY." *Codex, the Journal of the Louisiana Chapter of the ACRL* 4, no. 3 (2017): 64-82.

———. "Love, Sex, Disability, Coming Out, and John Travolta in New York and Jerusalem: A Twenty-Year Journey." *Graduate Journal of Social Science* 12, no. 1 (2016): 118-24.

Shklar, Judith N. *American Citizenship: The Quest for Inclusion.* Cambridge, MA: Harvard University Press, 1995.

Skyhorse, Brando, and Lisa Frazier Page. *We Wear the Mask: 15 True Stories of Passing in America.* Boston: Beacon Press, 2017.

Spina, Carli. "Libraries and Universal Design," *Theological Librarianship* 10 No. 1, October 2017, 5-7. https://theolib.atla.com/theolib/article/view/464.

Stone, Emma, and Mark Priestley. "Parasites, Pawns and Partners: Disability Research and the Role of Non-Disabled Researchers." *British Journal of Sociology 47*, no. 4 (1996): 699-716.

Swain, John, and Sally French. "Towards an Affirmation Model of Disability." *Disability and Society* 15, no. 4 (2000): 569-582.

Thomas, Carol. *Female Forms: Experiencing and Understanding Disability.* Buckingham, UK: Open University Press, 1999.

Thomas, Victoria L., and Lawrence O. Gostin. "The Americans with Disabilities Act: Shattered Aspirations and New Hope." *JAMA* 301, no. 1 (2009): 95-97.

Tucker, Bonnie Poitras. "The ADA's Revolving Door: Inherent Flaws in the Civil Rights Paradigm." *Ohio St. Law Journal* 62 (2001): 335.

US Department of Labor, Office of the Assistant Secretary for Administration and Management. *Section 504, Rehabilitation Act of 1973.* Accessed February 24, 2020. https://www.dol.gov/agencies/oasam/centers-offices/civil-rights-center/statutes/section-504-rehabilitation-act-of-1973.

Valeras, Aimee. "'We Don't Have a Box': Understanding Hidden Disability Identity Utilizing Narrative Research Methodology." *Disability Studies Quarterly* 30, no. 3/4 (2010). hhttp://dsq-sds.org/article/view/1267/1297.

Vernon, Ayesha. "A Stranger in Many Camps: The Experience of Disabled Black and Ethnic Minority Women." In *Encounters with Strangers: Feminism and Disability,* edited by Jenny Morris, 148-168. London: Women's Press, 1996.

Vernon, Ayesha. "Fighting Two Different Battles: Unity is Preferable to Enmity" In *Disability Studies: Past, Present and Future,* edited by Len Barton, and Mike Oliver, 255-262. Leeds, UK: Disability Press, 1997.

Vickers, Margaret. *Work and Unseen Chronic Illness: Silent Voices.* New York: Routledge, 2002.

Vornholt, Katharina ,Patrizia Villotti, Beate Muschalla, Jana Bauer, Adrienne Colella, Fred Zijlstra, Gemma Van Ruitenbeek, Sjir Uitdewilligen, and Marc Corbiere. "Disability and Employment–Overview and Highlights." *European Journal of Work and Organizational Psychology* 27, no. 1 (2018): 40-55. https://www.tandfonline.com/toc/pewo20/current.

Walker, Alice. "From an Interview," In *In Search of Our Mothers' Gardens: Womanist Prose.* 244-272. New York: Harcourt Brace, 1984.

Walker, Shaundra. "Critical Race Theory and The Recruitment, Retention and Promotion of a Librarian of Color: A Counterstory." In *Where Are All Librarians of Color? The Experiences of People of Color in Academia,* edited by Rebecca Hankins and Miguel Juárez, 135-160. Sacramento, CA: Library Juice Press, 2015.

Westkott, Marcia. "Feminist Criticism of the Social Sciences." *Harvard Educational Review* 49, no. 4 (1979): 422-430.

Wendell, Susan. "Unhealthy Disabled: Treating Chronic Illnesses as Disabilities." *Hypatia* 16, no. 4 (2001): 17-33.

———. *The Rejected Body.* New York, Routledge, 1996.

Williams, Patricia. "Spirit-Murdering the Messenger: The Discourse of Finger Pointing as the Law's Response to Racism." *University of Miami Law Review* 42 (1987): 127-157.

Wilson-Kovacs, Dana, Michelle K. Ryan, S. Alexander Haslam, and Anna Rabinovich. "'Just Because You Can Get a Wheelchair in the Building Doesn't Necessarily Mean That You Can Still Participate': Barriers to the Career Advancement of Disabled Professionals." *Disability and Society* 23, no. 7 (2008): 705-717.

Wolf, Naomi. *The Beauty Myth: How Images of Beauty are Used Against Women.* New York: Perennial, 2002.

World Health Organization. "Checklist of Essential Features of Age-Friendly Cities." 2007. https://www. who.int/ageing/publications/Age_friendly_cities_ checklist.pdf.

———. "World Report on Disability: Summary" 2011. https://www.who.int/disabilities/world_report/2011/ report/en/.

Zarb, Gerry. "On the Road to Damascus: First Steps towards Changing the Relations of Disability Research Production." *Disability, Handicap and Society* 7, no. 2 (1992): 125–38.

Appendix A

Charter for Compassion

The principle of compassion lies at the heart of all religious, ethical and spiritual traditions, calling us always to treat all others as we wish to be treated ourselves. Compassion impels us to work tirelessly to alleviate the suffering of our fellow creatures, to dethrone ourselves from the centre of our world and put another there, and to honour the inviolable sanctity of every single human being, treating everybody, without exception, with absolute justice, equity and respect.

It is also necessary in both public and private life to refrain consistently and empathically from inflicting pain. To act or speak violently out of spite, chauvinism, or self-interest, to impoverish, exploit or deny basic rights to anybody, and to incite hatred by denigrating others—even our enemies—is a denial of our common humanity. We acknowledge that we have failed to live compassionately and that some have even increased the sum of human misery in the name of religion.

We therefore call upon all men and women to restore compassion to the centre of morality and religion - to return to the ancient principle that any interpretation of scripture that breeds violence, hatred or disdain is illegitimate - to ensure that youth are given accurate and respectful information about other traditions, religions and cultures - to encourage a positive appreciation of cultural and religious diversity - to cultivate an informed empathy with the suffering of all human beings—even those regarded as enemies.

We urgently need to make compassion a clear, luminous and dynamic force in our polarized world. Rooted in a principled determination to transcend selfishness, compassion can break down political, dogmatic, ideological and religious boundaries. Born of our deep interdependence, compassion is essential to human relationships and to a fulfilled humanity. It is the path to enlightenment, and indispensable to the creation of a just economy and a peaceful global community.

www.charterforcompassion.org
https://www.charterforcompassion.org/charter/affirm

INDEX